COMRADE KROPOTKIN

COMRADE KROPOTKIN

VICTOR ROBINSON

ISBN: 978-93-5614-445-3

Published: 1908

© 2022
LECTOR HOUSE LLP

LECTOR HOUSE LLP
E-MAIL: lectorpublishing@gmail.com

Peter Alexeivitch Kropotkin

Born in the Old Esquerries' Quarter of Moscow in 1842

COMRADE KROPOTKIN

BY

VICTOR ROBINSON

"To liberate one's country!" she said. "It is terrible even to utter those words, they are so grand."

TURGENEV: "On the Eve."

1908

TO GEORGE KENNAN

I dedicate this work. I need not say why. He will know —
Everyone will know. With tears, during the night,
I have read your book, thou earnest truth-seeker.
O compassionate traveler, what a man you must have been!
For the weary Siberian exiles called you
'Dear George Ivanovich!' With a heart
Full of thankfulness for the work you have done,
I lay my bitter and bloody pages at your feet.

Victor Robinson

FOREWORD

Bernard Shaw calls us a nation of villagers. To a large extent this appellation holds good. We are so self-sufficient unto ourselves that the most important events in the world leave us cold if they take place outside of the realm of the star-spangled banner.

A wonderful and terrible thing is happening in the largest empire on earth; a downtrodden people is engaged in a death-grapple with its merciless rulers; and never were masters so inhuman, and never were people so heroic. In comparison with this titanic struggle the French Revolution itself sinks into insignificance. But what do we know about it? And what do we care? Russia is far away.... Once in a while the report of a particularly atrocious massacre, or a particularly cruel torture inflicted upon a young girl revolutionist will shock our sensibilities, will cause a pang in our hearts, will perhaps make our hair stand on end,—but in a day or two we forget all about it. We are so busy!

No wonder that this battle-drama appeals with special force, and exerts a special charm on the young of all lands,—the young who worship Freedom, and whose breasts beat warmly for Ideals. No wonder therefore that it appeals to Victor Robinson.

This essay was written at the age of twenty, and the youth of the author will serve as an apology, if apology be needed, for the sharpness of some of the expressions found in these pages. But is excuse really necessary? I hardly think so. No language can be too strong when condemning the Russian Bureaucracy, no judgment can be too severe when pronounced on czardom and its cruel minions. In fact the English language sometimes seems inadequate....

A remarkable commentary on the conditions in Russia is the fact that he who studies them carefully and thoroly, be he the gentlest and sweetest youth who would not harm a fly or tread on a worm, becomes saturated with the conviction that in Russia, the rebel's bomb and pistol and dagger are not only legitimate and necessary, but even noble weapons of defense and offense.

I refrain from any remarks as to the intrinsic value of this book, as it is perhaps not quite proper for a father to criticize, favorably or otherwise, the literary productions of his son. One comment however I would like to make: For one who is utterly unfamiliar with the Russian language, and who has worked alone and unaided, (in the leisure moments left over by strenuous college studies), the author has accomplished a rather noteworthy feat. He has succeeded in imbuing the book with such an atmosphere, in presenting such vivid and faithful glimpses of Russian life and literature, and exhibiting such wide and varied knowledge of the subject, that even a Russian writer would not be ashamed to have his name appear on the title-page of this volume.

Love understandeth all things.

DR. WILLIAM J. ROBINSON.

New York City, November 11, 1908.

CONTENTS

LIST OF ILLUSTRATIONS

UNDER NICHOLAS I.

I understand that doom awaits him who first rises against the oppressors of the people. When has Liberty been redeemed without victims? Fate has already condemned me. I shall perish for my native land. I feel it, I know it, and gladly bless my destiny.—*Ryleev.*

A fabled king of Thrace fed his horses on human flesh, but a real czar of Russia washed his streets with blood. On his accession to the red throne, the Iron Despot immediately expelled progress from his empire by butchering the Decembrists—those pioneers of freedom who fought for a constitution and the abolition of serfdom. Exiles began to tramp the lonely Siberian highway, and from the time of that Nicholas I. to this Nicholas II.—a period of 75 years—over a million political prisoners have taken the 'long journey.'

The mighty country was turned into a military camp. The term of service was twenty-five years. The life was so hard that when a man was recruited, his relatives followed him as if to his grave. His mother ran after him, and sometimes fell dead on the spot. The emperor spent his time reviewing troops and altering uniforms.[1] If an officer appeared in the streets with the hooks of his uncomfortable collar unfastened, he was liable to be degraded to the rank of a common soldier and deported to some distant province. If a soldier complained of his diet, or was guilty of the slightest infraction of the most insignificant rule, he was condemned to run the gauntlet. He was stripped naked, his hands were tied behind him, and he was brought between two long rows of pawing privates and eager 'non-coms,' equipped and armed with sticks, whips and gun-stocks. Behind the soldiers stood officers commanding, "Harder! Harder!" Thru these lines the victim was compelled to run—because in yesterday's paltry parade conducted by a petty sergeant, he scratched his itching neck. At first it was his shoulders which they struck, but before he had gone very far he had no longer a back, but only a bleeding mass of quivering flesh thru which parts of the bones protruded. A doctor was always present to see that the culprit did not die before receiving his full punishment. That is, if he were booked for 500 blows and was on the point of succumbing after receiving 300, it was the physician's duty to send him to a hospital to regain sufficient strength to allow the additional 200 to be administered. However, in spite of the medicus, the mangled men often perished before their time, and then there

---

[1] See "Russia," by Alfred Rambaud.

was nothing to do but beat the corpse.[2]

During this reign originated the widespread system of stealing Jewish children from their homes, separating them from their families, severing them from their faith, and bringing them up to serve in the army. These were the Cantonists.[3] Thus it came about that when a mother of Israel gave birth to a boy, she did not rejoice as for one born and living, but lamented as for one dead and departed. (Sometimes Jewish mothers saved their children from the army by cutting off their fingers, or taking out one of their eyes).

Liberty was so shackled she did not even dare weep aloud.[4] Since that unlucky day when Ryleev, Pestel, Bestuzhev, Kakovsky and Muraviov-Apostol dangled from a tall straight post and a strong crossbar, no revolutionist arose to oppose tyranny. During all the many years of the reign of Nicholas-with-the-Stick, no ray of light brightened a darkened nation, no torch glimmered in the bloody gloom. Hope was dead. Freedom was buried. Literature was in exile. Knowledge lay in a closed coffin. But censorship was alive, and autocracy had more eyes than Argus.

An anonymous pamphlet, toward the end of his reign, cried out that the czar had rolled a great stone before the door of the sepulchure of Truth, that he had

[2] Among those who witnessed this spectacle was Germain de Lagny, who describes it in his book, "The Knout and the Russians" ... "After fourteen hundred strokes, his face which had long before begun to turn blue, assumed suddenly a greenish hue; his eyes became haggard and almost started out of their sockets, from which large blood-colored tears trickeled down and stained his cheeks. He was gasping and gradually sinking. The officer who accompanied me ordered the ranks to open, and I approached the body. The skin was literally ploughed up, and had, so to say, disappeared. The flesh was hacked to pieces and almost reduced to a state of jelly; long stripes hung down the prisoner's sides like so many thongs, while other pieces remained fastened and glued to the sticks of the executioners. The muscles, too, were torn to shreds. No mortal tongue can ever convey a just idea of the sight.... It was seven months before he was cured and his health re-established; and, at the expiration of this period, he was solemnly taken back to the place of execution, and forced once more to run the gauntlet, in order to receive his full amount of six thousand strokes. He died at the commencement of this second punishment.... After all, Russia is only an immense barrack, in which every one is in a state of arrest." Yet the author of these words was a worshipper of Nicholas!

[3] They were called Cantonists because they were kept and trained in military settlements or cantons under Arakcheev. It is a most remarkable fact—considering the circumstance that they were taken away in early childhood—that several Cantonists who were able to live thru the horrors of the service, returned to their homes as orthodox and as fanatically devoted to their religion as if they had spent the preceding twenty-five years not in the military barracks of the gentiles, but in cheder and shool reciting the Torah.

[4] He slaughtered Poland like a hound tears a hare. "But below all (in the Museum of the Kremlin), far beneath the feet of the Emperor, in dust and ignominy and on the floor, is flung the very Constitution of Poland—parchment for parchment, ink for ink, good promise for good promise—which Alexander I. gave with so many smiles, and which Nicholas I. took away with so much bloodshed."—Andrew D. White, "The Development and Overthrow of Serfdom in Russia," Atlantic Monthly November 1862. This sentence which I have quoted is correct, but the reader who is unfamiliar with Russian history had better avoid the article, as the last paragraph alone contains as many lies as there are kalachi in Moscow.

placed a strong guard round her tomb, and in the exultation of his heart had exclaimed, "For thee, no resurrection!"

So thoroly was liberalism crushed, so completely was absolutism supreme, that 'Nikolaus Palkin' walked the streets of bleeding Russia unattended and unafraid.

Alas, when a nation has only knees to bend, but no hands to strike!

After his shadow had obscured the sun for a quarter of a century, a brilliant festival was given in his honor at Moscow—called the Holy City because it contains a Miracle Monastery for glorifying God and a Kremlin Fortress for crucifying Man. It was a fancy-dress ball, and a thousand gorgeous uniforms were there, from the leather coat of the Tungus to the embroidered flummery of the chamberlain. In this affair the children of the nobility played an important part. They were lavishly attired, and each carried an ensign representing the arms of the provinces of the Russian empire. At a given signal the little emblem-bearers began to march, and on reaching the purple platform upon which the royal family sat, all standards were lowered. The inflexible autocrat viewed the scene with satisfaction—all the provinces bowed before him. When the children retired to the rear of the immense hall, someone pulled the smallest of the boys from the ranks and placed him on the imperial elevation. The lad was arrayed as a Persian prince, and wore a jewel-covered belt and a high bonnet. Nicholas I. looked at his chubby face all surrounded with pretty curls and taking him to the czarevna Marie Alexandrovna, said in his military voice, "This is the sort of boy you must bring me." The woman was gravid at the time, and the soldier-like joke made her blush.

"Will you have some sweets?" asked the emperor.

"I want some of those tiny biscuits which were served at tea," eagerly responded the child. A waiter was called and he emptied a full tray into the tall bonnet.

"I will take them home to Sasha," said the curly little cherub.

Mikhael—the czar's brother—now paid attention to the little visitor. "When you are a good boy," he said, "they treat you so," and he passed his rough hand downwards over the rotund features of the diminutive would-be Persian; "but when you are naughty, they treat you so," and he rubbed the child's nose upward.

The poor innocent did his best to restrain himself, but unhappily the gushing tears could not be repressed. The ladies at once took his part, and Marie Alexandrovna set him by her side on a velvet chair with a gilded back—William Morris being then unknown. Soon the big eyes began to close, and drowsily putting his beautiful head in the lap of the future empress, the boy fell soundly asleep.

And the frolic went on. Under the glittering chandeliers the dancers glided. Over the waxen floors the merry feet waltzed. Wine disappeared by barrels, and revelry ran riot. Swords, spurs, buckles, medals, diamonds—how they all sparkled! The smooth-cheeked courtiers and the slick-tongued cavaliers gaily jested, and the silk-swathed ladies flirted their proverbial fans and smiled flatteringly at their wit, but not the wisest of them knew that someday this babe would awake and make his name terrible to the ears of tyrants!

SCENES FROM SERFDOM

> To be sold, three coachmen, well-trained and handsome; and two girls, the one eighteen and the other fifteen years of age, both of them good-looking and well acquainted with various kinds of handiwork. In the same house there are for sale two hairdressers; the one twenty-one years of age can read, write, play on a musical instrument, and act as huntsman; the other can dress ladies' and gentlemen's hair. In the same house are sold pianos and organs.
>
> Advertisement in the *Moscow Gazette*, 1801.

eter Kropotkin's father was a general and a prince. His family originated with a grandson of Rostislav Mstislavich the Bold. His ancestors had been Grand Princes of Smolensk. He was a descendant of the house of Rurik, and judged from the standpoint of heredity, had more right to the throne than the Romanoffs. Incidentally he was like most military men—barbarous, pitiless, merciless. He owned twelve hundred male serfs. We do not know how many maids. Neither do we know how many were scarred by the knout, how many were flogged till the breath of life left them, nor how many hanged themselves under his window.

If this brave warrior—who received the cross of Saint Anne for gallantry, because his servant Froll rushed into the flames to save a child—became imbued with the notion that there was not sufficient hay in the barn, he would call one of his serfs, strike him in the face, and accuse him of overfeeding the horses. In order to prove he was right he would make another calculation, and come to the conclusion there was too much hay. So he would bang his slave again for not giving the equidae enuf. Suddenly he would sit down and write a note: Take So and So to the police station, and let 100 lashes with the birch rod be administered to him.

On such occasions Peter would run out—his rosy cheeks wet with weeping—catch the unhappy soul in a dark passage, and try to kiss his hand. The serf would tear it away, and say bitterly, "Let me alone; you too, when you grow up, will you not be just the same?"

"No, no, never!" cried the child, while the hot tears choked him and made him cough for breath.

The females of all animals, having dislikes and preferences, exercise the right of selection; rejecting one and receiving another; sending away a male who is repulsive to them, and accepting a wooer they find attractive.[5]

[5] See Darwin's "Descent of Man."

Such absurd liberty was never allowed the serfs. They married when, where and whom the master wished. The Kropotkins owned a woman named Polya—intelligent and artistic—an exceptional serf. Her body was bound; her hands were doomed to labor; her talents brought benefits not to herself; her skill was at the service of others; her industry profited her owners; she was a chattel, chained and confined—but her heart could not be controlled. She deeply loved a neighboring servant, and was with child from him. The lover, forgetting the Russian proverb, "One cannot break a stone wall with his forehead," implored permission to marry her.... The Kropotkins owned also a dwarf called 'bandy-legged Filka.' Because of a terrible kick which he received in his boyhood, he ceased to grow. His legs were crooked, his feet were turned inward, his nose was broken, his jaw was deformed. It was the General's will that the refined Polya should wed this unsightly imp. She was forced to obey. The 'happy couple' were sent to the estate of Ryazan.[6]

During the sixth year of the reign of Alexander II., a servant dashed wildly into Peter Kropotkin's room. It was early in the morning, and Kropotkin was still in bed. But the servant brandished the tea tray and babbled excitedly, "Prince, freedom! The manifesto is posted on the Gostinoi Dvor." In a moment Kropotkin was dressed and began to run out. Just then a friend came running in. "Kropotkin, freedom!" he shouted, "Here is the manifesto!"

Kropotkin read it. His eyes beamed. He stamped his feet. O happy day! No more slavery—serfdom was abolished—the muzhiks were free. Not the dark ghosts of reaction, but the luminous sons of light had triumphed. Not Shuvaloff, Muravioff, and Trepoff, but Herzen, Turgenev and Chernishevsky.[7]

That afternoon Kropotkin attended the last performance of the Italian Opera. Baveri, the conductor of the band, raised his baton; the musicians began to play, but human voices drowned the notes, for the people were shouting for their czar—Redeemer!—Deliverer! Then Baveri stopped, but the hurrahs did not. Again Baveri waved his stick wildly in the air, the fiddlers grasped tightly their bows, the drummers beat with all their strength, the players inflated their lungs and blew the brazen instruments with might and main, but from that powerful band not a bar of music could be heard, for the people were shouting for their czar—Immanuel!—Illustrious! Strangers met in the streets, embraced, kissed each other thrice on the cheek, and shouted for their czar—Father!—Messiah! In front of the royal palace, peasants and professors mingled, and shouted for their czar—Emancipator!—Liberator! When he really appeared, crowds eager and immense, ran after

---

[6] Yet Kropotkin was not among the cruelest proprietors. To read what occurred on the estate of General Arakcheev is enuf to drive the stoutest mind insane. In the "Russki Archiv" is an account of a woman who by the most horrible tortures killed hundreds of her serfs, chiefly of the female sex, several of them young girls of eleven and twelve. Another woman murdered a serf boy by pricking him with a pen-knife, because he had neglected to take proper care of a rabbit. See Sir D. M. Wallace's "Russia." Also the "Memoirs of a Sportsman" and "Mumu" by Turgenev.

[7] Leonora B. Lang, who translated Rambaud's "Histoire de la Russie" from French to English, says there are about thirteen ways of spelling Patzinak. Ditto for Chernishevsky. The form which I have chosen is perhaps as proper as any, and simpler than most. An English reader is not supposed to be able to pronounce Tschernyschewskiy.

the carriage and shouted for their czar—Tsar Osvoboditel!

As a dream disappears at dawn, so died this enthusiasm. The brief moment of promise was followed by an eternal hour of despair; the short day was succeeded by the endless night. Hell may not be Hell, but a Romanoff is a Romanoff. Only one year later, the despot in Alexander awoke—mature and monstrous. If the dead could touch the living, Nicholas would have hugged his son. The steps of the scaffold became slippery with the blood of the best. The rope of the hangman was jerked day and night, and the key of the jailer creaked in a thousand locks. Reaction had won, and liberalism lay covered with a crimson shroud.

The Valuev volcano vomited its smothering lava as far as Siberia, and General Kukel who with Kropotkin's help was preparing a long list of necessary reforms, was dismissed from his post because another place had been found for him—in prison.

On the other hand there was a district chief who robbed the peasants and whipped their wives, and whose brutality and dishonesty were so unanswerably exposed by the energetic Kropotkin that this officer was also transfered—to a higher position in Kamchatka where he found more roubles for his purse and more women for his knout.

When Kropotkin returned to St. Petersburg on an official commission, a high functionary said to him, "Do you know that Chernishevsky has been arrested? He is now in the fortress."

"Chernishevsky? What has he done?"

"Nothing in particular, nothing! But *mon cher*, you know—state considerations!... Such a clever man, awfully clever! And such an influence he has upon the youth. You understand that a government cannot tolerate that: that's impossible! intolerable *mon cher, dans un Etat bien ordonné*!"[8]

For these mad acts of a drunken despotism, there was neither shadow of excuse nor shade of reason, except that a Romanoff was hungry and thirsty for victims, satisfying the blood-craving spirit that cried within him, demanding that the brightest youths and the noblest girls be changed to lifeless corpses.

Is it any wonder that men who on the great day of emancipation quoted with tears in their eyes the beautiful article by Herzen,[9] "Thou hast conquered, Galilean," now recited these other words by the same exile: "Alexander Nikolaevich, why did you not die on that day? Your name would have been transmitted in history as that of a hero."

---

[8] See P. Kropotkin's "Memoirs of a Revolutionist."

[9] For an account of Herzen's influence, see the "Russian Revolutionary Movement," by Konni Zilliacus. This excellent volume which all should read is of especial interest to Finns.

EXPLORATIONS

And at the same time falls upon his ear the plaintive song of the Russian peasant; all wailing and lamentation, in which so many ages of suffering seem concentrated. His squalid misery, his whole life stands forth full of sorrow and outrage. Look at him; exhausted by hunger, broken down by toil, the eternal slave of the privileged classes, working without pause, without hope of redemption. For the government purposely keeps him ignorant, and every one robs him, every one tramples on him, and no one stretches out a hand to assist him. No one? Not so. The young man knows now "what to do." He will stretch forth his hand. He will tell the peasant how to free himself and how to become happy. His heart throbs for this poor sufferer who can only weep. The flush of enthusiasm mounts to his brow, and with burning glances he takes in his heart a solemn oath to concentrate all his life, all his strength, all his thoughts, to the liberation of this population which drains its life blood in order that he, the favored son of privilege, may live at his ease, study, and instruct himself. He will take off the fine clothes that burn into his very flesh; he will put on the rough coat and the wooden shoes of the peasant, and abandoning the splendid paternal palace which oppresses him like the reproach of a crime, he will go forth "among the people" in some remote district, and there, the slender and delicate descendant of a noble race, he will do the hard work of the peasant, enduring every privation in order to carry to him the words of redemption, the Gospel of our age,—Socialism. What matters to him if the cut-throats of the Government lay hands upon him? What to him are exile, Siberia, death? Full of his sublime idea, clear, splendid, vivifying as the mid-day sun, he defies suffering, and would meet death with a glance of enthusiasm and a smile of happiness.— STEPNIAK: *Underground Russia.*

Peter Kropotkin came into life sailing on its topmost wave. The fat of the land, and its milk and honey were his. Personally, nothing was denied him. All the gifts had been lavished upon him. Position was his, health he had in abundance, he was as handsome as the characters in Tolstoy's *War and Peace*, and his talents were many and varied. To use the Russian vernacular, he was born in his shirt.

But not praise from princes or bows from beauties could induce him to fritter away his splendid energies in senseless dinky-dinks at Moscow or foppish balls at Petersburg. He wished to exercise head, hand and heart, for he agreed with John Ruskin that whatever else you are, you must not be useless and you must not be cruel—two adjectives which best portray the average official.

As has already been said, while still a youth Kropotkin went to Siberia to aid Kukel improve the prisons, the exile system, etc. But when the Herzen-reading Kukel was recalled, and it was no longer permitted to mention the word "reform," Kropotkin became an explorer.

Being clever, he soon made several important discoveries—the border-ridge of the Khingan, the tertiary volcanoes of the Uyun Kholdonsti, a direct route to the Amur.

Also it is interesting to remember that he was among the first Europeans who entered Manchuria,[10] and he went at the risk of being put in a cage and conveyed across the Gobi on a camel's back. It was impossible to go as an officer, so Kropotkin disguised himself as a trader, put on a long blue cotton dress, and acted like a Muscovite merchant—sitting on the edge of the chair, pouring his tea in the saucer, blowing on it with puffed-out cheeks and staring eyes, and nibbling tiny particles from his lump of sugar.

One night as he wandered thru a Chinese town, the inhabitants by signs asked him why such a young man wore a beard. Answering by the same means, Kropotkin told them that if he had nothing else to eat he could eat the beard. This caused the Celestials to roar with laughter, and they petted him tenderly, showed him their houses, and offered him more pipes than Skitaletz's Gavril Petrovitch could have smoked.

In 1866, Kropotkin found what previous explorers had vainly sought—a communication between the gold mines of Yakutsk and Transbaikalia.

Then came what he considers his chief contribution to science: the important discovery that the maps of Northern Asia were incorrect, because the main lines of structure run neither north and south, nor east and west, but from the southwest to the northeast.[11]

Later Kropotkin was to lead an expedition to the Arctic seas, but as the government was spending enormous sums in erecting scaffolds, it could not spare a poltinik for explorations in unknown regions. However the Geographical Society sent him to Finland to study the glacial deposits. Here he made valuable research-

[10] By P. Kropotkin: "A Journey from the Trans-Baikal to the Amur by Way of Manchuria," in the "Russian Messenger," June 1865.

[11] Not even Kropotkin's enemies have denied his scientific ability. Zenker, in his unfair and unsympathetic book on "Anarchism" says, "The dreaded Anarchist Kropotkin is and always has been active as a writer of geographical and geological works, and enjoys a considerable reputation in these sciences, apart from his activity as a Socialist teacher and agitator." The conservative Hon. Andrew D. White in his "Autobiography" calls him "one of the most gifted scientific thinkers of our time." The unbelievably cruel Pobedonostzeff—who would gladly have used the thumb-screws on him—refers to him as "a learned geographer and sociologist."

es relative to the glaciation of the country. He conceived the idea of writing a monumental physical geography of Northern Europe. His chief ambition was to become the Secretary of the Society, for then he would be in a condition to considerably advance the cause of science.

But because he now had more leisure than formerly, he began seriously to think of another subject—The People. When he crossed a plain which had no interest for a geologist, he thought of their sufferings. When he walked from one gravel pit to another, he mused on their downtrodden hopes. Sometimes the hammer would pause in mid-air before it struck the chisel, because the naturalist was dreaming of these plundered beings. After collecting an immense amount of evidence, he anticipated what keen joy he would have in analysing and arranging it for publication; but then another feeling would assert itself—what right had he to this happiness when all around him were men and women and children struggling and slaving for a bit of mouldy bread? Yes, yes, Kropotkin was thinking about the hungry people.

It was in the autumn of 1871, as he looked over the hillocks of Finland, and saw with his scientific eye the ice accumulating in the archipelagos at the dawn of mankind, that he received this telegram from the Geographical Society: "The council begs you to accept the position of secretary to the society."

At last Kropotkin was in a position to realise his old dream, but he pondered much before answering, for he now dreamed a new dream—how to lighten the burdens of the overworked people.

A voice in the wind said, "To work for Science is great."

Then another voice spoke saying, "To toil for Humanity is greater."

So Kropotkin wired, "Most cordial thanks, but cannot accept." The chisel of the geologist slipped from his fingers, and from that day on Peter Kropotkin carried in his upraised hand a burning torch for the weary people.

THE NIHILISTS

"He is a nihilist."

"What!" cried his father. As to Paul Petrovitch, he raised his knife, on the end of which was a small bit of butter, and remained motionless.

"He is a nihilist," repeated Arcadi.

"A nihilist," said Nicholas Petrovitch. "This word must come from the Latin *Nihil*, nothing, as far as I can judge; and consequently it signifies a man who ... who recognizes nothing?"

"Or rather who respects nothing," said Paul Petrovitch; and he began again to butter his bread.

"A man who looks at everything from a critical point of view," said Arcadi.

"Does that not come to the same thing?" asked his uncle.

"No, not at all; a nihilist is a man who bows before no authority, who accepts no principle without examination, no matter what credit the principle has." — Turgenev: *Fathers and Sons*.

It was a cheerless Saint Petersburg to which Kropotkin returned—a city in the grip of the powers of darkness. The officials despoiled the muzhiks of their last copecks, and if the poor peasants sought redress in institutions ironically known as "courts of justice,"[12] they were either imprisoned for life or murdered outright—at the order of the very men who were fleshed with pillage.

The best writers had escaped abroad, or languished in faraway Siberia, or had departed upon a still longer journey.

Where was Lavrov? Who heard of Mikhailov? What fortress held Pisarev? Why sat no ardent youths at Chernishevsky's feet?

The reformers who had worked for the abolition of serfdom were still. An uncanny fear possessed them. They trembled at the thought of Trepoff. They shuddered at the sight of Shuvaloff. They wished nothing but obscurity; they prayed only for oblivion to cover them. They denied with pale faces that they had ever held advanced opinions. They were a pitiful lot, but it is hard to blame them. Like

[12] "This court is worse than a house of ill-fame; there they sell only bodies, but here you prostitute honor and justice and law." —Ippolit Mishkin.

a blood-crazed beast Alexander roamed his empire, slaughtering human beings with a ferocity that would have made a pack of wolves protest. In the dead of the night they were shot—and sometimes at dawn. No reasons were assigned, no questions answered. Russia prostrated herself at the feet of power—poisoned with the fangs of force. Little wonder the old generation was frightened.

The lime had grown in their bones, and to have these bones crushed by Katkoff in the casemates of the Fortress of Peter and Paul was not pleasant. The fathers withdrew from the society of their sons. Even the older brothers held aloof. At every step the young people heard, "Prudence, young man." Never before was youth so deserted, and never before was youth so splendid, so supreme, so sublime. Was it for them to follow the craven footsteps of a cowardly generation? Let the overcrowded prisons answer! Let the youngster-jammed dungeons reply!

From the army came the young officer and cast aside his uniform. From the palace stepped forth the young prince and threw off his costly mantle. From the general's family hastened the young heiress and put away her silken dresses.

It is not for a halting tongue to celebrate this youthful band of pioneers. It is not for a faltering pen to chant praises to those whose glory is unrivalled. History has not seen their equals. They deserve the worship of a better world than this. We who have no faith in God or reverence for Government, may well bow our heads at the recollection of men who left comfortable firesides to expose themselves to maddening tortures. We may well fall right down on our knees at the thought of women who bade farewell to wealthy parents to bare their breasts to the sabre of the gendarme and the embrace of the cossack.

Authorities they rejected. The chains of custom they rent asunder. Even the axiomatic they re-examined. With the luke-warm, half-hearted agnosticism of Huxley, they were dissatisfied. Out-and-out apostles of Atheism were they, and one of the first books they printed was Ludwig Buchner's. The theory of transformism they eagerly accepted, and more than any English evolutionist they would gladly have died to prove Darwin right and Cuvier wrong.[13]

Only one mistake they made—they spat upon Art. They found no joy in beauty. An arched rainbow, a Grecian urn, a vine-covered cottage, were nothing to them. They scorned the laurels of the golden-haired Apollo. They claimed a shoemaker was superior to Raphael because he makes useful things while the other does not.

---

[13] If the reader has not read Stepniak's "Underground Russia" he should do so without delay.

The Scaffold's Bride

It is for such girls that the czar buys rope.

Their sacred watchword was: To The People. This great movement—which Turgenev[14] named Nihilism—spread rapidly. Many schools were established and enormous numbers of peasants flocked to them. The old sat on the benches with their grandchildren and did their best to learn. Teachers and the taught were enthused with the great idea. Leaders and the led were comrades. The youths did not spend a couple of hours with the peasants and then run off to indulge in an abnormal orgy prepared by a pathic Grand Duke. Altho several were heirs to fortunes, they refused to accept any money from their parents. They lived exactly like the peasants, several in a room, ate black bread and dressed in boots and sheepskin. Many of the girls formerly owned a trunkful of jewels and a houseful of servants, but now they dispensed with chignon and crinoline. They cropped their hair close and put on blue spectacles so they might not be fair in the eyes of men. They wanted no love affairs. They wanted to educate the ignorant. Children of the rich, offsprings of aristocrats, scions of nobility, brought up in luxury, encouraged in idleness, unused to manual work, unaccustomed to physical labor, they now toiled fifteen hours a day in the factories. To look peasant-like, the prettiest maidens rubbed their cheeks with grease and steeped their hands in brine. All the woes of the commoners they accepted for themselves. Were there ever before such luminous sons, such divine daughters? Ask history for a parallel, and Clio's scroll is blank!

Let this statement stand—indeed not even the twisted intellect of the perverted W. T. Stead[15] could demolish it—had the autocracy permitted these young teachers to continue their educative work among the peasants, Russia to-day would not be a nation of illiterate muzhiks, and millions who are now hopelessly blind would have eyes that see.

---

[14] See his "Fathers and Sons," but avoid the abominable translation by Eugene Schuyler. To the eternal honor of the nihilists it must be said that they instantly and emphatically repudiated the hero of this novel, the brutal Bazarov. I myself have no hesitancy in saying that I prefer even the perfumed dandy Paul Petrovitch, to this harsh, coarse, repulsive, insulting individual who treats his loving parents like dogs, and who refers to a beautiful woman by exclaiming, "What a magnificent body! How fine it would look on a dissecting table!" Here is one of the curiosities of literature: a great artist conceives a great admiration for a great type, and yet he produces—a caricature! But Kropotkin seems to have a somewhat higher opinion of Bazarov, for in a letter which I received from him, he says, "Those Nihilists who understood Bazarov as Pisarev did, were right. Those who reproached Turgenev for Bazarov's scorn to work for mankind were right again. Turgenev has not succeeded in representing the man of action whom he admired well enough to excite the uninitiated admiration of the reader." For a correct representation of a nihilist in a novel—which the nihilists themselves heartily accepted—see the character of Rakmetov in Chernishevsky's wonderful "What is to be done?" Among those who enthusiastically praised this work was Sophia Perovskaya.

[15] The English eulogist of Russian officialism, the hypocrite who is intimate with Nicholas II., the scoundrel who praises Trepoff, and yet speaks of uplifting humanity!! He has written a lying book, "The Truth About Russia."

THE TERRORISTS

In July 1906, I was in Bialystok. A pogrom had just been started. I saw women who were repeatedly raped before the eyes of their husbands and their fathers. I saw a child, four years old, deliberately shot in the arm by a soldier. I saw a girl of twelve shot in the stomach. I saw a hospital that was purposely fired upon by soldiers merely to create a panic among the patients. The local schoolmaster was killed by three gendarmes driving nails into his skull. The whole reason for the massacre was to terrify the population into submitting meekly to various governmental impositions. The massacre is a recognized weapon of the Russian Government, often used to shape political ends. By what standards of the eternal verities is it wrong to combat this kind of slaughter by removing the official or officials responsible? To assassinate an Alikhanov, a Pavlov, a Min, a Dubossov, a Sergius, a Plehve, is, to my mind, precisely like killing a rattlesnake that has crawled into a nursery, or stamping out a pest, or blowing up a building to stop the further spread of the flames.

KELLOGG DURLAND: *The Necessity for Terrorism in Russia.*

It is not often remembered — tho it should be — that at this time these Nihilists were not politicals, and did not fight czarism. Their object was to teach the alphabet, not to overthrow the dynasty. It was only when the government condemned to a slow death in Siberia every one who printed a leaflet, or distributed a pamphlet, or attended a meeting, or listened to a speaker, or joined a co-operative association, or started an experimental farm, or went to a technical school, or taught a peasant — that they commenced to oppose the Romanoff regime. It was only when the ultimatum, "No schools allowed!"[16] was for several years rammed down their

---

[16] This fact is so notorious that even an obscurantist like W. R. Morfill must admit it. See the passage in his mediocre book, "Russia." But illiberal as this work is, it at least is not outrageous. What however are we to do with Augustus Hare ("Studies in Russia") who writes that exile to Siberia is pleasant; with Rev. Henry Landsell ("Through Siberia") who informs us that punishment with the knout was not painful; with Miss Annette Meakin ("A Ribbon of Iron") who describes the cruel Gribsky as a kindly man; with John A. Logan ("Joyful Russia") who is religiously convinced that the czar is an angel; with Francis H. Skrine ("Expansion of Russia") who approves the worst crimes of the house of Romanoff. Of course lackeys are always plentiful, but how sad that Russian Despotism should have Anglo-American defenders.

throats at the point of the bayonet that the Nihilists became Terrorists. It was only when the prisons overflowed with their young warm blood that Sophia Perovskaya waved her handkerchief.

The shaft of truth is naked, and so armored with bias is the mind of man, that the missle cannot pierce the mail. In spite of the unanswerable array of historical data, many will still exclaim, "We do not believe in using force in Russia. We believe in education."

O huge Sviatogor, giant-hero of the primitive Russians, endow us with your mighty nerves, lest we burst!

There was a girl—Miss Gukovskaya. A young girl—fourteen years old.[17] She addressed a crowd—about Kovalsky. She was transported to a remote part of Siberia for life. The child could not endure the wilderness and drowned herself in the Yenisei.

There was another girl who gave a single pamphlet to a worker. Her punishment was nine years of hard labor and then life-long exile among Siberian snows.

A young man was found reading a book not admired by the censor. He was put in prison and kept there until he committed suicide.

When the gay and gentle Starinyevitch was a student, a manifesto was found in his possession. Unwilling to incriminate another, he refused to say from whom he received it. For this omission he spent twenty years in filthy prisons.

While searching the room of Rosovsky who was not yet twenty, the police discovered a proclamation of the Executive Committee.

"Who gave it to you?"

"That I cannot say. I am not a spy."

He was sentenced to death and died on the scaffold.[18]

Kropotkin mentions another youth of nineteen who posted a circular in a railway station. He was caught and killed—hanged I think. "He was a boy," says Kropotkin, "He was a boy but he died like a man."

Ask a Revolutionist if he knows Sophia Bardina and his glowing eyes will answer yes. Because she read a couple of articles in public, she was condemned to several years' penal servitude, which by special favor of the czar was commuted to life-long exile.

Leo Deutsch in his mild and modest *Sixteen Tears in Siberia*, tells of a few girls of Romny who hit upon the plan of loaning one another books and making notes on them. Soon a few young men joined, and thus was formed a small reading society, such as might help to pass away the long winter evenings in the dull provincial town. For this—and for absolutely nothing but this—"the conspirators of Romny" were deported across the Urals.

---

[17] Russian heroines begin early. The renowned Vera Zasulitch was just sweet sixteen when she startled the world by shooting and wounding the murderous General Trepoff.

[18] See "Russia Under the Czars," by Stepniak.

Only a couple of years ago, several schoolteachers met at Tiflis to discuss the best method of improving their educational curricula. A commander entered and cried, "Disperse!" Turning to his cossacks he said, "These women are yours"—and all were raped with impunity.

As long as the Romanoffs rule Russia, only idiots opaque and impervious to reason, can speak of education without action.

If education were permitted, revolutionary violence would not be, because terrorism is the last straw to which the drowning nation clutches. They cling to this because under existing circumstances nothing else is possible, nothing, nothing, nothing.

Russia has produced no greater Terrorist than Gregory Gershuni, and when this glorious Jew stood before his "judges" he told them: "History will forgive you everything; the centuries of oppression, the millions you have starved to death, the other millions you have sent to be butchered on the battlefield; everything but this—that you have driven us who mean well with our fatherland to seek recourse in murder."[19]

---

[19] This is the sentiment of all Russian Rebels. When the beautiful revolutionary nurse, Anna Korba, was on trial, 1882, she said, "If the party of the Will of the People adopts the policy of terror, it is not because it prefers terrorism, but because terrorism is the only possible method of attaining the objects set before it by the historical conditions of Russian life. These are sad and fateful words, and they bear a prophecy of terrible calamity. Gentlemen—Senators, you are well acquainted with the fundamental laws of the Russian Empire. You are aware that no one has a right to advocate any change in the existing imperial form of Government, or even to think of such a thing. Merely to present to the Crown a collective petition is forbidden—and yet the country is growing and developing, the conditions of social life are becoming day by day more and more complicated, and the moment approaches when the Russian people will burst thru the barriers from which there is no exit." Here she was interrupted by the presiding judge, but continued, "The historical task set before the party of the Will of the People is to widen these barriers and to obtain for Russia independence and freedom. The means for the attainment of these objects depend directly upon the Government. We do not adher obstinately to terrorism. The hand that is raised to strike will instantly fall if the Government will change the political conditions of life. Our party has patriotic self-control enuf not to take revenge for its bleeding wounds; but, unless it prove false to the Russian people, it cannot lay down its arms until it has conquered for that people freedom and well-being." One of the last things that Stepniak tells us in "King Stork and King Log" is: "Terrorism is the worst of all methods of revolutionary warfare, and there is only one thing that is worse still—slavish submissiveness, and the absence of any protest."——An unusually good editorial, "The Meaning of Terrorism," appeared recently in the New York Evening Post, in which it was correctly said, "In exchange for freedom of self-expression, the Revolutionists stand ready instantly to abandon terror, and they point for proof of their sincerity to the cessation of warfare during the period when the Duma was being elected and sat, to their readiness even now to suspend hostilities for the coming elections; small reason tho they have for confidence in the future plans of the government."——The Boston Herald (March 16, 1905), in a column editorial called "How Assassins Are Made," says, "The dark cloud of Russian oppression is riven only by thunderbolts. There is no wind of free speech to drive it away."——The editor of Altruria (November 1907) in answering a gentleman who objected to terrorism in Russia, writes, "When he says 'there are other ways,' he is mistaken. That's all. That is just the trouble. In Russia

Men cannot meet for purposes of discussion, because if they do, they will be beaten and bayoneted. Children cannot, for they will be hacked to pieces. Women cannot, for their bodies will be utilized to warm the beds of cossacks.

Such liberticide must be answered by tyrannicide! And the hand that holds a dagger, red with the blood of a despot, is the noblest hand of all!

there are no other ways; not at present. There was hope of peaceful reformation; the Government destroyed that hope. The bomb and the bullet, therefore remain the only weapon."

SOPHIA PEROVSKAYA

All the condemned died like heroes. Kibalkitch and Geliabov appeared very calm and resigned. Timothy Mikhailov pale but firm; Rysakov calm and under control, but his face was as white as a sheet. Sophia Perovskaya's courage struck us all with astonishment. Not a sign of fear of death in her lovely countenance. Her cheeks wore the fresh roses of youth and health, and a heroine's soul gleamed from her gentle, but firm and serious face.

—From the reactionary Kolnische Zeitung.

Russia has long been famous for its circles, which far surpass in interest and excellence, those of any other country. According to the calculation of the police, each member contributes to the society either a pint or a quart of blood, but this computation is too conservative. Those who join Russian Circles do not measure the amount, but are ready to give unto the last drop. At these meetings, chairmen and ceremony are unknown. Those present sit on chairs, lean against the window-sill, or squat on a broken sofa. They sing melancholy songs, smoke cigarettes and overwork the samovar. They dress carelessly in loose blouses of colored calico. Their hair is disheveled, their faces are flushed, their eyes are blazing. All argue at once, and in order to make themselves heard, interrupt each other, shout animatedly, bang the table, and rattle the spoon in the glass. The noise is deafening, but from the din of the debate fly forth sparks which may eventually inflame even this outraged empire of officials and icons.

In 1872, Kropotkin joined the most important of these groups—the Circle of Chaykovsky. Kropotkin was now a thoro-going revolutionist, and it is foolish to ask as Grand Duke Nicholas did, "When did you begin to entertain such ideas?"

Nicholas Chaykovsky

"The Father of the Russian Revolution."

In a country like Russia, where the present government incites the troops to massacre the people, hoping in this way to prolong its existence;[20] where the wardens do a thriving business by turning over the female prisoners to the soldiers at so much a piece; where the Dnieper-Demons beat women to the ground and ride their horses over their bosoms; where they toss children in the air and catch them on their bayonets;[21] where they hack babes in twain and hurl the bleeding pieces at their agonized mothers; where they hammer spikes thru the heads of old men;[22] where youths are exiled for life for reading a forbidden author; where vulgar officers command refined women to become their mistresses[23] or pay the penalty of having their families shipped to that side of the tear-drenched monument which says, "Asia;" where officials who plan pogroms are promoted, and those who protest are imprisoned[24] where tortures like pricking out the eyes[25] and striking the stomach are perpetrated; where virgin and matron are used to glut the lust of the cossack;[26] where such crimes are openly committed from dawn to dusk and thru the darkness of the black night, that at mere thought of them the suffering brain reels, and the horrified senses faint—in a land like this could a Peter Kropotkin remain Chamberlain to the Czarina?

Such rare-souled characters formed this Circle, that Kropotkin spent here the two happiest years of his life. To pass whole days with Nicholas Chaykovsky, to speak with the Kornilov sisters, to work with the young Kuprianov, to grasp the

[20] See the book on massacres by the ex-bureaucrat Prince Urusoff, in which the high official shows that the government itself is the chief pogrom-preparer. Translated by Herman Rosenthal.

[21] See "Within the Pale," by Michael Davitt. Also Bialik's "'Al Shechitah," either in the Jewish Quarterly Review or The Maccabean, January 1907. Translation by Helena Frank.

[22] See the "Report of the Duma Commission on the Pogrom at Bialystok," published in the London Jewish Chronicle, July 1906. Reprinted in its entirety in the American Jewish Year Book, 1906-1907. At Kishineff, the wife of Fanorissi Siss had nails driven thru her eyes. See also Book II of "Gillette's Social Redemption," and Kropotkin's letter in the London Times, July 25, 1908.

[23] See "Russia from Within," by Alexander Ular. This truthful volume contains many horrible revelations concerning the fearfully cruel and corrupt Grand Dukes.

[24] For a well-edited "Table of Pogroms" see American Jewish Year Book, 1906-1907. Out of hundreds of examples, here is one: On the last day of October 1905, a frightful carnage overtook the Jews in Odessa. Their financial loss amounted to at least one million rubles, and six thousand of them were killed and injured. The Self-Defense was well organized, but when they fought too valiantly, the police surrounded them and shot them down. The janitors were ordered to point out Jewish flats to the mob. An imperial Ukase was published, thanking the troops for their excellent work. Nineteen officers who tried to prevent the wholesale butchery were transfered to obscure posts, while Neidhardt who was Prefect of Police at this time was promoted to the position of Governor of Nishni-Novgorod. I purposely quote very modern instances, so English readers will see that the crimes of the Romanoffs are not things of the past.

[25] See "The Revolution in the Baltic Provinces." The author's name is withheld for obvious reasons, but the terrible little book is edited by J. Ramsay MacDonald, a well-known member of Parliament. The reader of nervous temperament will not find the chapter on the "Torture Chambers of Riga," at all enjoyable.

[26] For numerous instances see the "Red Reign," by Kellogg Durland. From every standpoint this is one of the most admirable works that has appeared on Russia.

honest hand of Stepniak, to enter the room at night in top-boots after lecturing to peasants, and see sweet Sophia Perovskaya say severely, "How dare you bring so much mud in this house!"—what life could be intenser?

The Circle of Chaykovsky held its meetings in a little dwelling in the suburbs of Saint Petersburg. There was nothing about it to excite suspicion. The neighbors often saw the mistress attending to her business. They knew her to be an artisan's wife, an ordinary workingwoman. She wore a cotton dress and men's shoes, her head was covered with a fancy kerchief, and she trudged slowly along, carrying on her shoulders full pails of water from the Neva River.

But they did not know that she belonged to the highest aristocracy; that one of her ancestors was the morganatic husband of Empress Elizabeth, daughter of Peter the Great; that her grandfather was Minister of Public Instruction; that her uncle was a renowned conqueror in Asia Minor; that her father was Governor General of St. Petersburg; that she herself had shone in the most fashionable drawing rooms of the capital, and that her name was Sophia Perovskaya,—a name which thrills the soul of every rebel to its center.

Physically she was like a novelist's heroine. She had golden hair and her eyes were blue. A lissom figure, a musical voice, a charming laugh.[27] Pure with a maiden's modesty, chaste with a virginal shyness. So graceful and girlish that she never looked more than eighteen—even when she was twenty-six. Of such a sympathetic nature that when she became a nurse, sufferers whose nerves quivered in distress, claimed their agony abated as soon as she entered. Her mother she loved to adoration, and often at the risk of her life, she left her hiding-place to give Varvara Sergyevna the joy of folding her hunted child in her aching arms. Her father had human form, but was in reality a fiend, yet rejoice that he lived, for from his ultra-reactionary loins was born the white queen of the red revolution.

From her sixteenth year, Sonya was ready to die for the Cause—with a smile on her beautiful lips and a wave of her graceful hand, with the crimson banner above her head, and upon her bosom a red carnation. I speak figuratively. She would not have worn these things. She was altogether too simple.

Hers was a life full of pain, and in 1881 came the supreme sorrow. Her heart twitched with the torture, for Andrew Geliabov, the man she loved so fondly, was in the casemate of the fortress, and all knew, and Sonya knew too, that soon around his beloved neck would be a bluish streak. Yet her brilliant intellect was not dimmed or darkened. That will of iron and those nerves of steel, neither broke nor faltered. It was then that she arranged every detail for the assassination of Alexander II. She may have wept in private, but to her comrades she said with dry eyes, "When I give the signal, throw the bomb."

The appointed day came. In a metal-clad carriage, the czar drove to the pa-

[27] "She had the ready laugh of a girl, and laughed with so much heartiness, and so unaffectedly, that she really seemed a young lass of sixteen.... At dinner time, when all met, there was chatting and joking as tho nothing was at stake, and it was then that Sophia Perovskaya—at the very moment when she had in her pocket a loaded revolver intended to blow up everything and everybody into the air—most frequently delighted the company with her silver laugh."—Stepniak.

rade. Behind him in a sledge rode Colonel Dvorjitsky. Burning eyes looked at a girl. A handkerchief fluttered in the air—Sonya's signal! Rysakov threw his bomb. The Emperor alighted—unhurt. Then Grinevetsky too, flung a blessed ball of Kibalkitch's make, and within a few hours the old despot and the young martyr passed out of the world.

Sophia Perovskaya inspired the greatest stanzas of the Poet of the Sierras, for usually the verse of the slangy Joaquin Miller is mediocre. But how grand are these!:

> "A storm burst forth! From out the storm
> The clean, red lightning leapt,
> And lo, a prostrate royal form ...
> And Alexander slept!
> Down thru the snow, all smoking, warm
> Like any blood, his crept.
> Yea, one lay dead, for millions dead!
> One red spot in the snow
> For one long damning line of red,
> Where exiles endless go—
> The babe at breast, the mother's head
> Bowed down and dying so.
>
> And did a woman do this deed?
> Then build her scaffold high,
> That all may on her forehead read
> The martyr's right to die!
> Ring Cossack round on royal steed!
> Now lift her to the sky!
> But see! From out the black hood shines
> A light few look upon!
> Lorn exiles, see, from dark, deep mines,
> A star at burst of dawn!...
> A thud! A creak of hangman's lines!—
> A frail shape jerked and drawn!..."

Before stepping upon the scaffold, Sophia Perovskaya wrote a note. (I know it has often been printed, but how can I help publishing it again?) Think you she laments that one so gifted should perish so young? Read:

"Mother, mother! Beloved, beloved one! If you only knew how cruelly I suffer at the thought of the sorrow and torture I have caused you, dearest—! I beg and beseech you not to rack your tender heart for my sake. Spare yourself, and think of all those who are round you at home, and who love you no less than I do—and need you constantly; and who, more than I, are entitled to your love and affection. Spare yourself too, for the sake of me, who would be so happy if only the agonizing thought of the sorrow I have caused you did not torture me so unspeakably. Sorrow not over my fate which I created for myself, as you know, at the strict behest of my conscience. You know that I could not have acted differently, that I was obliged to do what my heart ordered, that I had to go and leave you, beloved mother, when my country called me. Do not think that the death that inevitably awaits me has any terror for my soul. That which has happened is only, you know, what I have been expecting every day, every hour, during all those years, and what sooner or later, must overtake me and my friends. Soon, in the course of a few days, I must die for the cause, for the idea, for which I devoted my life and all the powers of my soul and body. How happy I should be then, dearest, beloved! Once more I beseech you not to mourn for me. You are well aware how ineffably I love you, I have always, always, loved you. By this love I conjure you to forgive your Sonya! Again and again I kiss your beloved hands, and on my knees, thank you for all you have given me during every moment of my life. On my knees I beseech you to bear to all the dear ones at home my last loving greetings! To-morrow I shall stand once more in the presence of my judges; probably for the last time. But my clothes are so shabby, and I wanted to tidy myself up a bit. Buy and send me, dearest mama, a little white collar and a pair of simple loose sleeves with links. Perhaps it will be vouchsafed us once again to meet. Till then, farewell! Do not forget my last fervent prayer, my last thought: forgive me and do not bewail me."

Yes, this is her letter. "Buy and send me, dearest mama, a little white collar and a pair of simple loose sleeves with links."

A woman still—but glorified, radiant, resplendent—a woman all inspired, upraised, exalted, uplifted, aureoled.

Sophia Perovskaya

She was hanged in her twenties, but her name is as immortal as the eternal sun.

THE FORTRESS OF PETER AND PAUL

A strange feeling came over me when I saw that I was being conveyed to this prison, used by the Government of the Czars for political offenders only; a place never spoken of in Russia without a shudder. —LEO DEUTSCH: *Sixteen Years in Siberia.*

he Circle of Chaykovsky exerted an immense influence all over the empire, forming branches in every province, and producing the greatest of the Russian Revolutionists. Yet the particular group to which Kropotkin belonged was daily decreasing, on account of the imprisonment of its members.

In January 1874, the police became so vigilant that the remaining comrades thought it wise for Stepniak to leave St. Petersburg. But this noble and lovable giant, whose simplicity earned him the epithet of "Baby," refused to obey. He protested warmly, and remained at his risky post until the Nihilists actually forced him to depart to a safer city.

It was also time for Kropotkin—who had become famous by his speeches to the 'prostoi narod'—to conceal himself, but in his case a strange circumstance prevented. He had just completed his essay on the glacial formations, and it was necessary to read it at a meeting of the Geographical Society. When he finished, an animated discussion began, but laurels were on Kropotkin's head; it was admitted that all old theories concerning the diluvial period in Russia were erroneous. This paper produced such an excellent impression that it was proposed to nominate the author president of the Physical Geography section. So Kropotkin sat among the fine gentlemen, and shook hands with the dignified professors, and smilingly thanked the learned savants for the honors they conferred upon him, but inwardly he asked himself if he would not spend that very night in the prison of the Third Section.

His guess was not a bad one. He was soon arrested. After certain tedious formalities, he was put in a cab. A colossal Circassian sat at his side. The genial Kropotkin spoke to him, but the mass of meat only snored. Many of Kropotkin's comrades were already entombed in Litovsky prison, but his question if he too were going there was unanswered. Then the cab crossed Palace Bridge, and it was no longer necessary to interrogate the guardian. Peter Kropotkin knew he was bound for that silent coffin of stone which darkly rises like a Hell-on-Earth—the Fortress of Saint Peter and Saint Paul.

He leaned over and looked at the flowing Neva, knowing he would not soon see the graceful river again. Over the gulf of Finland, clouds were hanging, but the prisoner searched for patches of blue sky. The sun was going down, wearily perhaps, but proudly, for as it slowly sank below the horizon it left behind it gossamer colors of sapphire and scarlet, with glint and glow of gold. (And the officer snored.)

The carriage turned to the left and entered a dark passage. Kropotkin was now within the gate of the Cemetery for the Living, the mouldy, murderous Tomb of Torture. Thru his mind flashed all the horrors of this famous prison whose dreaded name is uttered only in a voice hushed and awed.[28] Within these walls the Decembrists became martyrs. Here Nechaev—in the gloomy Alexis ravelin[29]—was kept a prisoner for life. Here Perovskaya had been confined. Here was incarcerated the poet-prince Odoevsky, about whose early death the banished Lermontov wrote so tender an elegy.

The carriage stopped before another gate which was opened by soldiers. Here Catherine II.[30] buried alive all who opposed her abominations. Here the terrible Minich tortured his enemies until they expired from the agony. Here Princess Tarakanova was locked in a cell which filled with water, causing the rats to climb upon her body to save themselves from drowning. Here in the awful loneliness of the silent dungeons, an army of unfortunates had gone insane.

The carriage rested again and Kropotkin was taken to a third iron gate which opened into a dark room where he could vaguely see several soldiers in soft felt boots gliding noiselessly about as if they were phantoms from another world. He recalled that here was caged much of the winged glory of Russian Literature— Ryleev, the poet of freedom whose forbidden ballads Kropotkin's mother copied in her note-books; Griboyedov who wrote one immortal masterpiece[31] and then put pen no more to paper because the censor mutilated his work beyond recognition; Shevchenko who dipped his quill in a soul of tears and wrote heart-breaking poetry about his fellow-serfs; Dostoyevsky, the sensitive novelist who described so well the injured and insulted; Pisarev, a truly marvellous critic whose voice was a trumpet-call arousing the youth to a higher life; Chernishevsky, the profoundest thinker of his time, as great a genius as the race of man has produced.[32] These— and how many more!—had spent weary years in the fortress where he was now walking.

---

[28] See the "Memoirs of a Revolutionist."

[29] See the "Russian Bastille" by Simon O. Pollock in the International Socialist Review, March 1907.

[30] If anyone cares to know to what sexual depravities royal ladies can descend, let him read what Dr. W. W. Sanger says about Empress Elizabeth and the two Catherines in his valuable "History of Prostitution." The number of lovers they caressed was surpassed only by the number of thinkers they tortured. The first-named had a reputation for humaneness. Does this mean that during her reign no one was exiled? No, it means that during her reign only 80,000 of her subjects were knouted and deported to Siberia.

[31] Prophetically named "The Misfortune of Having Brains." (Gore ot Uma).

[32] For a brief but sympathetic sketch of Chernishevsky by one who knew him personally, see the "Russian Revolt" by Edmund Noble. It contains this sentence: "Such was the cost of trying to be a Cobden or a Bright in Russia!"

He remembered that in one of these cells the dauntless Karakozov was frightfully maltreated by being deprived of sleep. The gendarmes, who were changed every two hours, were ordered to keep him awake. Karakozov was inventive, and as he sat on his small stool he would cross his legs, and swing one of them to make his tormentors believe he was up; meanwhile he would steal a nap, continuing to swing his leg. When the gendarmes—depraved, imbruted blood-spillers—discovered the deception, they shook him every few moments whether he swung his limb or not. It is also quite certain that all his joints were crushed, for when he was taken out from the fortress to be hanged, he looked like a lump of rubber or heap of jelly. His head, arms, legs, trunk, were altogether loose as if they contained no bones or only broken ones. It was terrible to see the strenuous efforts he made to ascend the scaffold.

Kropotkin was taken to another black hall where armed sentries were moving. He thought of the mighty Bakunin, who was kept in an Austrian prison chained to the wall for two years, and then spent six more in this Fortress of Peter and Paul, and yet came out as fresh and pink as a boy.

He was put into a cell—a casemate originally intended for a cannon. A heavy oak door was shut behind him, a huge key turned in the lock, and the prince who had slept in the lap of an empress, who had been petted by Nicholas I., and who as sergeant of the corps of pages became the closest personal attendant of Alexander II., was left alone in a darksome reduit.

The prisoner examined his cell. High up in the granite wall a hole was cut. Kropotkin dragged his stool there, looked out and listened. Emptiness—no sound. He tapped the walls—no response. He struck the floor with his foot—no reply. He spoke to the sentry—no answer. The coldness, the dampness, the darkness were bad enuf, but this utter silence, this intense stillness, this grave-like deadness were maddening.

No human being addressed him; no living thing held intercourse with him—except the pigeons which came morning and afternoon to his window to receive food thru the grating. Only the bells of the fortress cathedral were heard. Every quarter of an hour they chimed to the glory of Jesus, and every midnight they pealed forth, "God save the Czar."

Then all was mute ... and nothing more....

Not only did no one speak to him, he was not even permitted to speak to himself. When the killing silence first began to oppress him, he hummed a tune. Then the spirit of song took hold of him, and he raised his voice. He sang from his favorite opera, Glinka's *Ruslan and Ludmila*—"Have I then to say farewell to love forever?"

"Sir," said a bass voice thru the food-window, "do not sing!"

A few days later, Peter Kropotkin could not sing.

BROTHERS

o time crept on with crippled feet, halting and limping on its broken crutches, held back by heavy ball and clanking chain. Thru the five feet of granite the sun could not penetrate, but grief came in thru the mortar. No oxygen passed the Judas, but with noisy wings sorrow flew in the embrasure. The oaken doors held freedom out, but sadness passed the bars of iron.

A great blow came to Kropotkin. He heard news which sickened him. Life lost its meaning. His stool remained unused in the corner.[33] All the day long, and during the endless hours of night, he wandered up and down his cell like a dazed animal. Friendly faces could not see him, but distress was his warder, and despair became his familiar visitor. He had learnt of the arrest of his brother Alexander[34]—the Sasha for whom he had saved the tiny tea-cakes.

The history of Peter Kropotkin can never be written and the name of Alexander left out. Tho only a year older, Sasha was in advance of him intellectually. This alone shows what a remarkable child he was, for Peter also was precocious: at twelve he dropped his title of prince, signing himself merely P. Kropotkin; at fourteen he wrote articles in favor of a constitution; and while still at school, he became the author of a text-book on physics which was printed for the use of his

---

[33] Determining to preserve his physical vigor, Kropotkin mapped out for himself a course in gymnastics. Among other feats, he made excellent if undignified use of his weighty oak stool. He balanced it on his nose and lifted it with his teeth; he put it on the end of his foot and raised it at right angles to his body; he turned it on its edges and twirled it like a wheel; he tossed it from one hand to the other, faster and faster; and he hurled it between, under, and across his legs.

[34] That is, his arrest in 1875; for Alexander Kropotkin had previously been arrested and thrown into prison in 1858, for reading Emerson's essay on "Self-Reliance," which was loaned to him by a university professor. For a portrait and his noble behavior on this occasion, see George Kennan's world-known "Siberia and the Exile System."

class-mates.

But more than anyone else, it was Sasha who opened unknown vistas to him, who stimulated his mind, who guided his studies, and directed his reading.

"What happiness," wrote Kropotkin many years later, "it was for me to have such a brother! To him I owe the best part of my development."

However, we soon forget Sasha's abilities—great as they were—in the contemplation of his white soul, of his spotless character, of his open heart, of his affectionate and exceptional personality.

When he grew to manhood, he departed from Russia. His spirit was too lofty to exist in this blood-soaked hell of ghoulish czars. He needed freedom like the eagle needs the mountain crag. Had he shared his brother's views, he would have remained to work and die for the Cause. But as it was his opinion that a popular uprising was an impossibility, he could take no part in political agitation, and he went to Switzerland with wife and child. Here his great scientific work assumed monumental proportions; it was to be a nineteenth century counterpart of the renowned *Tableau de la Nature* of the Encyclopædists. He labored in love, for science was to him what it was to Darwin.

Then he heard of Kropotkin's arrest. In a twinkling he left everything. He re-entered the gore-dripping cave of the Bloody Bear. For his loved brother's sake he breathed again the murderous miasma. Once more he walked in that cursed country where the nagaika of the cossack beats freedom to death.

Better than anyone else, he knew that if Kropotkin could not write, he would die. The Geographical Society and the Academy of Sciences wished the prisoner to finish a volume on the glacial period, and using this as a support, Sasha petitioned the authorities to allow his brother resume work. He made every scholar in the capital miserable, and plagued every scientific association until they agreed to support his application.

The fruit of this labor was that the governor entered Kropotkin's cell bearing precious gifts. It would take an Ippolit Mishkin in his most eloquent moment to describe the captive's unfathomable joy when he felt the paper beneath his palm and clutched in his hungry fingers, an inked pen!

In the presence of gendarmes, the brothers were permitted to see each other.[35] Sasha was much agitated. He hated the very sight of the uniforms of the executioners, and was too frank to keep his feelings to himself. Kropotkin was happy to see his honest face, his eyes full of love, and yet he wished him as far away as Zurich, for he knew that tho Sasha now came to the Third Section by day of his own free will, the time would come when he would be brought there by night under the escort of blue-garbed gendarmes.

Kropotkin was right. Sasha wrote a letter to his friend, the famous refugee and profound thinker, P. L. Lavrov, in which he mentioned his fears that his brother will fall ill in his armored chamber.

The Third Section intercepted the letter and arrested the writer. This was the

[35] See Kropotkin's "Memoirs of a Revolutionist."

story which leaked into Kropotkin's cell and broke him down.

"Before the Search"—By Kolinichenko

A Russian student burning his papers.

There is a touching little poem by Nora Perry about two attractive young ladies who come home after the ball. It is late, and they sit on the bed in their pretty nightgowns, stockingless, slipperless, combing their beautiful hair. Their dresses and flowers and ribbons are scattered over the room. They talk of the evening's revel, and laugh idly at the waltz and merry quadrille. Yet the hearts of these girls are not quite as light as their lips, for they both love one man and they fall asleep dreaming of him—his face shines out like a star. Here the poetess leans over the alluring sleepers and whispers if they could but peep into the future, they would not be jealous of each other, for ere another year rolls by, one will be ready for bridal and the other for burial. The eyes of one will sparkle among her jewels; her cheeks will blush thru her curls, but the other will be in that cabalistic country where there is neither wish nor want.

Yet is it not well that we cannot lift the mysterious veil and peer behind the darksome curtain? Otherwise would not we see future tragedies that would rob us of all strength to live thru the present?

Certain it is that had Kropotkin guessed the fate that was to befall Sasha, he would soon have left the fortress—carried out.

It may be a mooted point as to whether cossacks or gendarmes have been more successful in violating women, but all will agree that the former are pre-eminent in sabering students, while the latter receive the palm when it comes to searching houses. When half a dozen of them, accompanied by an officer,[36] burst into Sasha's flat after midnight, on Christmas eve, they excelled themselves. Against Alexander Kropotkin there was no accusation except that he had written a personal letter to a personal friend. Yet the Third Section kept him a prisoner for several months.

At this time his charming child, whom illness rendered still more affectionate and intelligent, was dying from consumption. It was not Sasha's nature to ask favors from his enemies, but when Death beckons with its bony finger, one cannot be proud. So Sasha asked permission to see his son for the last time. The request was refused. He begged to be allowed to go home for one hour, promising on his word of honor to return. The request was refused. Then the high-souled man cast his spirit in the dust before them and implored to be taken there in chains, and guarded by gendarmes. The request was refused.

The child died; the mother went half mad with grief; Sasha was told he would be transported to one of the loneliest towns in farthest Siberia; that he would travel in a cart between two gendarmes; that his wife could not go with him, but might follow later.

A year passed, and Sasha remained in exile. Another year, and he was still

[36] "There is not depicted in Russian literature a single type of officer which inspires sympathy or commands respect."... "Each of these young officers knows a string of such anecdotes all relating to the same topic. Here we have a tipsy cornet who rushes among a crowd of Jews and scatters them with drawn saber. A sublieutenant sabers a student who had inadvertently jogged his elbow. An officer shoots dead a civilian who had ventured the remark that a gentleman never addressed ladies to whom he had not been introduced."—G. SAVITCH in La Revue.

in Siberia. His sister Helene, without asking anyone, wrote a petition to the czar. She gave it to her cousin Dmitri Kropotkin, an unfeeling scoundrel who was afterwards killed by the revolutionist Goldenberg. At this time he was governor-general of Kharkoff, aide-de-camp of the emperor, and a favorite of the court. Heartless as he was, he thought it unjust for a non-political to be exiled so long, and he handed the petition personally to Alexander II., adding words of his own in support of it. Romanoff took the document and wrote upon it:

"Let him remain there."[37]

Ten years later. Sasha was still in bleak Siberia, cut off from his scientific work, severed from the intellectual world. A gloomy night—the wolves howled and Sasha lived. But these things could not go on forever. A silent night—the wail of the wolf ceased, and the soul of Sasha escaped.[38] Helene wrote no petitions to Death, but it was Death that liberated him.

---

[37] This is a typical drop in the ocean of his extreme cruelty.—Among those who contributed to my "Symposium on Humanitarians," (see August 1908 issue of the Medico-Pharmaceutical Critic and Guide), was the distinguished ex-ambassador to Germany and Russia, Andrew D. White, Ph.D., L.H.D., LL.D. He mentioned as one of his favorites, Alexander II. Naturally I could not understand such a barbaric choice. A little later, this eminent former President and Professor of Cornell University published his "Autobiography," and I found he was the apologist, admirer and friend of Pobedonostzeff! He speaks as highly of this relentless persecutor as of Leo Tolstoy! I deserve to have my face slapped for expecting Truth and Right from an official personage!

[38] He committed suicide by shooting himself.

THE OPEN GATE

The autumn night is dark as the crime of the traitor. But darker still, piercing the mist like a gloomy vision, stands—the prison. The sentinels are striding idly around, and in the deepness of the night is heard their groanlike melancholy "Lis-ten!" Tho the walls of the barrier are strong, tho the iron locks are unbreakable, tho the eyes of the gaolers are keen, and everywhere are shining bayonets, still the prison is not a morgue. Thou sentinel, be not negligent, trust not the darkness, be careful, Lis-ten!... MIKHAILOV.

The plague of the prisons was upon Kropotkin—he was sick with scurvy[39] and dying from insufficient oxidation of the blood. The wretches who lifted the shutter of the Judas and spied upon him, believed he would soon change his silent casemate for a silent coffin.

His relatives heard about his condition, and their alarm was great. His sister Helene tried to obtain his release on bail, but the procureur turned himself like a golden pheasant and said with a sinister smile, "If you bring me a doctor's certificate that he will die in ten days, I will release him." The girl fell in a chair and sobbed aloud. Shubin smiled again, for like Gorky's Tchizhik in *Orloff and his Wife*, he was fond of gratuitous entertainments.

But a prince is not a peasant, and Kropotkin was examined by a thoroly competent physician who ordered his transfer to the military hospital (where politicals were sent when it was thought they would soon require an undertaker).

Kropotkin improved at once. With a full chest he breathed the blest air which he had missed so long. The rays of the sun warmed him, and the scent of flowers gladdened his life. The immense window of his spacious room may have been grated, but it was never closed. He sat there all day gazing at the rows of trees.

---

[39] For a description of this disease, see Professor Osler's "Principles and Practise of Medicine."——"In parts of Russia scurvy is endemic, at certain seasons reaching epidemic proportions; and the leading authorities upon the disorder, now in that country, are almost unanimous, according to Hoffmann, in regarding it as infectious."——This reference to a physician reminds me of an interesting little book which has just appeared, "Glimpses of Medical Europe," by Dr. Ralph L. Thompson. Writing of Russia he says, "In St. Petersburg are fine parks and theatres and comfortable hotels in abundance. But despite it all there is an odd feeling of oppression that strikes one the moment he lands on Russian soil, and one doesn't breathe freely till he is out of it all."... "Personally I wouldn't mind foregoing health, friends and money, to fame; but if it came to a question of living in Russia, I would choose to die unknown."

Later he was taken out for an hour's walk in the prison yard—large, and full of sweet growing grass. The first moment he entered it, he stopped on the doorstep unable to move. Before him was a gate, and it was open! He tried not to look at it, yet stared at it all the time.

The desire of the moth for the flame, the attraction of steel for loadstone, the bond between chlorine and hydrogen, the affinity of kalium for the halogens—what are these compared to the passion of a prisoner for an open gate?

Kropotkin trembled as if in a fever. From head to foot his body shook, while the heart leaped and his pulses throbbed. He soon managed to let his Circle know how near he was to liberty, and immediately the comrades determined to aid him in escaping. Plans and plots were devised and disposed of, till Kropotkin feared all would be too late. He violated the rules of hygiene, hoping to keep in bad health, for he knew his walks would be stopped as soon as the doctor pronounced him well. Alas! in spite of all his efforts, his weight increased, his eyes brightened, his complexion cleared, his digestion improved. All symptoms of scurvy left him,—the livid spots under the skin and the oozy spongy gums disappeared.

At last all was ready. The revolutionists were sentimental, and decided the escape should occur June 29th, Old Style, for this is the day of Peter and Paul. It was arranged that Kropotkin's signal that all was well should be the taking off of his hat, and if all were right outside, the comrades would send up a red toy balloon. The day of the "saints" came. At the usual time—four o'clock—Kropotkin was brought out for his walk. He took off his hat, and waited for the little balloon. But in the air no red ball arose, and at the end of an awful hour, he returned to his cell—sick, crushed and broken.

A peculiar thing had happened. Usually hundreds of balloons could be bought near the Gostinoi Dvor. Yet that day not a red one was seen—only blue and white ones were there. Later one was discovered in the possession of a child, but it was damaged and could not ascend. The comrades rushed into an optician's shop, bought an apparatus for making hydrogen, and filled the rubber with the gas. Had they pumped it full of fluorine, the result would not have been worse. No inflation occurred, and the unexpanded balloon did not fly—but time did. The comrades grew worried. Then a lady attached the useless toy to her umbrella, and holding it above her head walked along the prison wall. But Kropotkin saw nothing because the wall was high and the lady was short.

The next day, at two, another lady came to the prison, bringing Kropotkin a watch. Not dreaming that a pocket time-piece could contain anything dangerous, the authorities passed it along without examination. Kropotkin did not look at the hour, but pulled off the lid, and found a tiny cipher note containing a new plan. (Had one of the officials performed this operation the lady's life would have been forfeited.)

This time the comrades rented the bungalow opposite the hospital. A musician was there ready to play on his violin if all were well. For a mile around every cab had been hired to render pursuit difficult. But what was to be done with the soldier who was posted at the gate and who could easily prevent Kropotkin from gaining the street, by merely stepping in front of him with lowered bayonet? Ah, the comrades, like Chitchikoff in Gogol's *Dead Souls*, had an idea. This soldier had once worked in the laboratory of the hospital, and therefore they appointed one of their number to divert his attention by a discussion on microscopes.

At four o'clock Kropotkin was escorted to the yard. He waited a moment, wiped his brow as if it were hot, and took off his hat. From the little gray house a violin sounded. The tones fell sweetly on Kropotkin's ears. He moved toward the gate intending to run in a moment. Suddenly—the music ceased. His heart hurt. Something writhed. One painful minute passed ... Two ... Three ... Four ... Five ... Ten minutes ... No music ... A quarter of an hour.... Some heavily loaded carts entered the gate, and Kropotkin understood the cause of the interruption.

Immediately the violin trilled. Kropotkin listened with interest. The musician was talented, and performed with much feeling. You felt that if three of the strings broke, like Paganini he would still make ravishing music on the fourth. Moreover his technique was perfect. He was playing a mazurka from Kontsky—wild, eager, thrilling,—a mad mazurka. It attracted Kropotkin like a magnet. It pulled him to the end of the footpath. He trembled lest it should stop again, but the intoxicated sounds floated over the prison yard, louder and louder, with ever-increasing passion and freedom.

Kropotkin glanced at the sentry. This hero followed a line parallel to his, but five paces nearer the gate. He was supposed to walk directly behind the prisoner, but as Kropotkin always crawled feebly along at a snail's pace, the able-bodied sentry who was too vigorous to creep, hit upon the above device.

Five paces nearer the gate—that was bad. But the sentry was only a sentry, while Peter Kropotkin was a mathematician and a psychologist. He calculated that if he began to run, the soldier instead of heading directly for the gate to cut off his escape, would obey his natural instinct and endeavor to seize him as quickly as possible. He would thus describe two sides of a triangle, of which Kropotkin would describe the third alone.

Fortissimo—how loudly that violin played! Kropotkin ran!

No sooner had he taken a few steps than some peasants who were piling wood, shouted, "He runs! Stop him"! It was for the people that Kropotkin was in prison; it was for them that he descended from his high estate; it was for them that he was ready to die at any moment. But the blocks with the slanted brows did not understand. At night when they lay on their rotting straw, they thanked the good gods for sending them such good masters. Now they called out, "Stop him! Stop him!"[40]

When Kropotkin heard that cry, he fled with a speed equal to Commandant Masyukov's, when Madame Sigida struck him. Already the sentry—doing just what Kropotkin expected him to do—was at his heels. Three soldiers who were sitting on the doorstep, followed. The athletic sentinel was so confident he could

[40] For a work dealing with revolutionary workmen and peasants, see "Mother," by Maxim Gorky. See also the admirable "Russia's Message" by William English Walling. This book is illustrated with magnificent photographs, including the latest one of Kropotkin.

outrun the invalid that he did not fire, but flung his rifle forward, trying to give the fleeing patient a bayonet-blow in the back. But it is never safe to take chances with even a sick runner, when he is sprinting for his life.

"Did you ever see what a big tail that louse has under the microscope?" asked the scientific comrade of the soldier at the gate.

"What, man! A tail? Why, man, you're crazy!"

"That's right. It has a tail as long as that."

"Come man, none of your tales now. Do you take me for a fool? I know a thing or two about the microscope myself."

"But I tell you it has. I aught to know better. That's the very first thing I saw under the microscope."

At this moment Kropotkin ran past them unnoticed, and tho usually much interested in convex lenses, took absolutely no part in the animated argument.

On gaining the street he was dumfounded to see that the huge man who occupied the carriage wore a military cap. The unhappy thought came to him that he had been betrayed. But on running nearer he saw it was a friend.

"Jump in! Jump in!" cried this modern Mikoula Selaninovich in a terrible voice, calling him a vile name. Leaning over to the coachman, he shoved a revolver in his face, screaming, "Gallop! Gallop! I will kill you, you— —!!" using language abusive enuf to have made every foul-mouthed cossack in the cavalry stare in mute admiration.

Springing into the air from a forefoot, the beautiful horse—a famous trotter named Barbar—flew along as if it were shod not with steel but with wings. When the cause of Revolution is triumphant, this flying quadruped should receive a statue of purest gold, for two years later it rendered another magnificent service to the movement by bearing to safety the Nihilist Stepniak, after he helped assassinate the monstrous Mezentsov—murderer of many.[41]

Like lightning it leapt thru a narrow lane; they entered the immense Nevsky Prospect; they turned into a side-street; Kropotkin ran up a stair-case; the smiling comrade-coachman drove away. At the top of the steps waiting with painful anxiety was his sister-in-law. Physiologists claim it is impossible to do two things at one instant, but Kropotkin says that when he fell into her arms, she laughed and cried at once, and at the same time bade him change his clothes and crop his beard. Ten minutes later, he and his muscular Mikoula left the house, and took a cab.

---

[41] The Russian Revolutionists are too modest. Stepniak in "Underground Russia," finds it necessary to mention that Mezentsov was stabbed to death in the streets of Saint Petersburg in full daylight, but he does not tell the reader that he himself was the author of the glorious deed. To find this out, we must go to another work; for instance, Konni Zilliacus's "Russian Revolutionary Movement," or Leo Deutsch's "Sixteen Years in Siberia," (see the English translation by Helen Chisholm). On the other hand Deutsch escaped in a romantic manner from the prison in Kiev, but in his book he refers to it so casually that if we wish to learn the facts we must go to another work; either Stepniak's, or Professor Thun's "Geschichte der revolutionaren Bewegung in Russland."

About an hour after, the house was searched, but as Kropotkin was not there, and it was necessary to arrest someone, the police took his sister and his sister-in-law.

Kropotkin was puzzled where to spend the time till evening, but his big friend knew. He called out to the cabman, "To Donon!" which has the same significance in Saint Petersburg that Delmonico has in New York, or Cecil in London, or Doree in Paris, or Bristol in Berlin, or Sacher in Vienna.

The decision was wise, for the police searched the dirty slums, but not the swell West End. So Kropotkin, dressed in an elegant costume, entered the aristocratic restaurant, and as he walks thru the halls flooded with light and crowded with guests, let us fill the biggest bumper with the richest wine, and quaff congratulations to the noblest prince that was ever imprisoned—and escaped.

Then softly let us retreat on tiptoe, and glance at his products for the bookshelf.

FROM THE PRINTING PRESS

> You poets, painters, sculptors, musicians, if you understand your true mission and the very interests of art itself, come with us. Place your pen, your pencil, your chisel, your ideas at the service of the revolution. Figure forth to us, in your eloquent style, or your impressive pictures, the heroic struggles of the people against their oppressors, fire the hearts of our youth with that glorious revolutionary enthusiasm which inflamed the souls of our ancestors; tell women what a noble career is that of a husband who devotes his life to the great cause of social emancipation! Show the people how hideous is their actual life, and place your hands on the causes of its ugliness; tell us what a rational life would be, if it did not encounter at every step the follies and ignomies of our present social order. —P. Kropotkin: *An Appeal to the Young*.

eter Kropotkin's writings range from obscure articles in unknown papers read by a handful of faithful subscribers, to cloth-bound far-famed volumes translated into several languages; include contributions to periodicals as revolutionary as *Revolte* and as respectable as the *Atlantic Monthly*; embrace all subjects from machinery to music, and from Tolstoyism to Terrorism.

Judged from a literary standpoint, his work is distinctly disappointing. It is styleless. But it has one redeeming feature: clearness. The man is straight. He is not ashamed of his ideas. He speaks right out. He is one of the few authors who writes for the peculiar purpose of being understood. He does not bury the flower of his thought in a wilderness of words.

It cannot be contended that Kropotkin gave up his style because he writes for workers who are unable to appreciate the beauty of literary composition. A man may refuse a title with an oath as Carlyle did, or give it up as Kropotkin himself did, but he who has a style relinquishes it not, for this is a gift besides which the 'boast of heraldry' is as a puppy's snappish yelp unto the lion's mighty roar.

Neither can it be claimed that Kropotkin's stylistic deficiency is due to the fact that he is an economist. So was Henry George, and yet there is a magical music in *Progress and Poverty* which makes the phrases flow like a poem of Pushkin's.

Nor can it be argued that his style has been spoilt by the circumstance that he writes in various languages, for in none of his work is there epigram, imagery or imagination—the glorious trinity of the stylists. But what has a foreign tongue to do with it? Was not Kossuth just as much an artist in English as in his native pepper? Even when he cried that we must seize the opportunity by the *front hair*? Many waters cannot quench love, and strange alphabets do not wipe out style.

What is a stylist? He is one who handles words, who licks phrases into shape, who moulds clauses to his bidding, who compels a sentence to leave a deathless impression, who weaves a connected chain of harmony from the scattered links of language.

Kropotkin has written very much, but practice does not make a stylist any more than learning the rules in the *Rationale of Verse* makes one capable of producing *The Raven*. The secret of style is revealed to few. Its essence is a mystery in which only a handful are initiated. The elusive occultism of art consists in this—that a single expression has the power to either damn a passage into oblivion, or to emblazon it forever in eternity.

To give a striking instance: When Edgar Poe first wrote *To Helen*, these lines composed the second stanza:

> "On desperate seas long wont to roam,
> Thy hyacinth hair, thy classic face,
> Thy Naiad airs have brought me home
> To the beauty of fair Greece,
> And the grandeur of old Rome."

In this case the concluding couplet is cheap and commonplace—"fair Greece" and "old Rome" being anemic expressions unfit to live. Poe amended it to read:

> "To the glory that was Greece,
> And the grandeur that was Rome."

Miracle of Art! This is not a change, but an apotheosis. We now have two lines which lay before us in gorgeous perfection a picture of the past; two lines as splendid as they were sickly, as magnificent as formerly they were mediocre. Yet the idea is the same in both cases. What then is it which makes so much difference? It is the manner of expression—it is style—it is art.

There is no reason why one man should be a stylist and another should not, but so it is. Huxley was a stylist; Darwin was not; Herzen, yes; Kropotkin, no.

Being anxious to know Kropotkin's exact attitude towards Art, I wrote to him asking categorically: "In your opinion, have exquisite poets like Keats and Pushkin—who never touched social questions, but celebrated only beauty—been of much benefit to mankind?"

He answered thus: "Not in a direct way, but perhaps *very much in an indirect way*: Pushkin by creating language,[42] and Keats by teaching love of nature. As to "exquisiteness," have we not had too much of those egotistic sweets?"

Closely analysed, and reduced to its ultimate elements, this answer shows

---

[42] When Pushkin began to write, the Russian literary language was in a somewhat unsettled and nebulous state, and his poetry helped to form and fix it. He thus did for Russian literature what Chaucer did for English.

that Kropotkin has no use for art per se. According to him Keats and Pushkin are benefactors not because of their beautiful verses, but because of other reasons. Exquisiteness he condemns altogether. He rejects the doctrine of Art for the sake of Art. He does not subscribe to the creed of Flaubert, Gautier, Bouilhet, Maupassant, Anatole France and Lafcadio Hearn.

I think Kropotkin is wrong, and I believe that because his work lacks artistic finish, much of it is doomed to perish.

Maxim Gorky, in speaking of a brief period when the Russian Censorship was somewhat suspended, said, "Books fell over the land like flakes of snow, but their effect was as sparks of fire!"

If Kropotkin wished to express the same idea, he would say it something like this: "Numerous books of all descriptions were published and distributed thruout Russia."

How fine Gorky's; how poor Kropotkin's. How vivid the former; how weak the latter. This is the difference between style and lack of it. Not in the entire range of Kropotkin's writings is there a single sentence in any way comparing with the above one of Gorky's; for he who writes without art holds a crippled pen. I may be mistaken, but in my opinion this single quotation from the Bitter One is worth all Kropotkin's *Freedom Pamphlets*. It is sublime in its similes and exquisite in its antitheses. There is a power in it which unchains enthusiasm and awakens intensity. "Books fell over the land like flakes of snow, but their effect was as sparks of fire." It is art. It is unforgettable, while to remember a phrase from *Modern Science and Anarchism* is impossible.

With this introduction, we may proceed to examine his work, much of which is necessary and valuable, tho none of it is of primal or epoch-making importance. Stepniak is right when he says, "He is not a mere manufacturer of books. Beyond his purely scientific labors, he has never written any work of much moment." And as Herzen said of Ogaryov, we may remark of Kropotkin: "His chief life-work was the working out of such an ideal personality as he is himself."

The majority of prominent periodicals in England and America to which Kropotkin has contributed, are listed in the *Reader's Guide* which can be found in any library, and those interested can look them up. Of course, many of these articles are first-class, but I can stop to mention only two. See *Russia and the Student Riots* (*Outlook*, April 6, 1901), which deals with the disturbances which caused the young revolutionist, Peter Karpowitch, to kill Bogolepov, Minister of Public Instruction. It shows with painful clearness the extreme and useless savagery of that cruel, repulsive, Stead-praised, arch-murderer, Nicholas II.

See also the *Present Crisis in Russia*, (*North American Review*, May 1901). In this excellent essay he refers to the Procurator of the Holy Synod in these words: "Pobedonostzeff, a narrow-minded fanatic of the state religion, who—if it were only in his power—would have burnt at the stake all protestants against Orthodoxy and Catholicism."[43]

---

[43] Kropotkin is too mild. Pobedonostzeff, world-renowned as the "Modern Torquemada," shed more blood, and was a colder and—if possible—crueller being than the ter-

Who should answer this article, but Pobedonostzeff himself! (*Russia and Popular Education*, N. A. R. September 1901). How strange when Light and Darkness are arrayed against each other![44] Pobedonostzeff calls Kropotkin "a learned geographer and sociologist;" but says; "Tho a Russian, he (Kropotkin) does not understand Russia, and is incapable of understanding his country; for the soul of the Russian people is a closed book to him which he has never opened." It is noteworthy that he does not attempt to deny Kropotkin's charge that if it were only in his power he would burn at the stake all protestants against orthodoxy and catholicism. Doubtless he considers this his chief crown of glory.

There was a further response from Kropotkin, (*Russian Schools and the Holy Synod*, N. A. R. April 1902).

Among his pamphlets which are used assiduously by the anarchists of all countries for propaganda, and which often cause the arrest of the devoted distributer, are: *Anarchism: Its Philosophy and Ideal. The State: Its Historic Role. War. Law and Authority. The Paris Commune. Organized Vengeance—called Justice. Anarchist Communism: Its Basis and Principles. An Appeal to the Young. The Psychology of Revolution. The Wage System.* These tracts are valuable as eye-openers to uneducated workmen, but they possess no merit whatsoever for cultured liberals.

Altho Kropotkin has written more than thirty geographical articles for the *Encyclopedia Britannica*, it is difficult to think of this revolutionaire as a contributor to this backward publication. The *Encyclopedia Britannica* is not on the trail for truth—it wants current prejudices. For instance, Professor Samuel Davidson, D. D., LL. D., was asked to contribute an essay on the *Canon*. Happening to be a scholar as well as a theolog, the venerable man was not satisfied with the logic of Father Irenaeus, that since the earth has four corners, and there are four winds, and animals have four legs, there must be four Gospels. His article was so mutilated by the editors of the *Encyclopedia*, that in justice to himself, he was obliged to publish the original version in book form, *The Canon of the Bible*. When the *Encyclopedia* mentions liberty, it is from the reactionary viewpoint. The *American Supplement* follows its parent in this respect, for here are eulogistic accounts of the second and third Alexanders, by Nathan Haskell Dole.[45] This literat is so ignorant of the most rible Spanish Inquisitor, while the physical tortures that he used, with the exception of burning at the stake which was too open an affair, were practically the same that were in vogue during the Dark Ages. He started numerous massacres which resulted in the deaths of great numbers. He often inflamed peoples who lived in harmony, to destroy each other. He was eminently successful in stirring up racial hatred and religious prejudice. "When I was in the Caucasus I saw the Georgian everywhere working peacefully and contentedly side by side with the Tartar and the Armenian. How happily and simply, like children, they played and sang and laughed, and how difficult now to believe that these simple, delightful people are busy killing each other in a senseless, stupid way, obedient to dark and evil influences."—Maxim Gorky in London Times. These "dark and evil influences" emanated from the medieval fissures in the theologic brain of Constantine Petrovitch Pobedonostzeff.

[44] Twenty years previous, in the pages of this very magazine, the same thing occurred, for the enlightened Ingersoll and the orthodox Jeremiah Black argued about Christianity.

[45] We would naturally expect better things from the author of that specially fine sonnet, "Russia" (see Stedman's American Anthology), beginning:

important epochs in the Russian Revolution, that he writes, "Vera Zasulich murdered General Trepov;" when all the world knows that Trepov was only wounded and soon recovered.[46] Luxuriously abound the weeds of his misstatements.[47] He speaks of the 'private virtues' of Alexander III. They must have been very private indeed, for no one ever discovered them. He speaks of his 'noble aspirations,' but the son of Maria of Hesse-Darmstadt had only this one aspiration: to wipe out freedom as effectually as a whirlwind blows away a puff of smoke. Such is the famous publication to which all school-girls resort when they must prepare a composition on Milton.

Kropotkin's strictly scientific works, the *Orography of Asia* and the *Glacial Period* were written in Russian and have not been translated into English.

During his imprisonment at Clairvaux, appeared his *Words of a Rebel*, 1885, in French, published by Elisee Reclus. It is a critical exposition of Anarchism.[48]

In 1886 he published his first book in English, *In Russian and French Prisons*. This work soon disappeared from the market. Kropotkin himself offered a high price for a copy, but could not obtain one. It seems the agents of the Russian government bought up the entire edition and destroyed it.

In 1892 appeared his *Conquest of Bread*, in French, which has been translated into Dutch, German, Spanish, Portuguese, Norwegian, English. It is perhaps his most important work and has been much reviewed and quoted. Notice to those who wish to think: Study this volume.

In 1898 appeared his *Fields, Factories and Workshops*. This highly excellent work is the splendid outcome of several essays which were written a decade previous for the *Nineteenth Century* (1880-1890), and one for the Forum, (*Possibilities of Agri-*

> "Saturnian mother! why dost thou devour
> Thy offspring, who by loving thee are curst?"

[46] The same mistake (and a respectable number of others) is made by William Eleroy Curtis in his false and disgusting "The Land of the Nihilist." He devotes a whole chapter to Alexander II., speaks continually of his assassination, and yet does not know even the name of the famous assassin. He says it is Elnikoff (sic)! This is a bad guess. On this occasion two bombs were thrown. The first by Rysakov, and it destroyed the carriage. The second by Grinevetsky, and it destroyed the emperor. How carefully and conscientiously the well-informed author has studied the history of the Russian Revolution which he so vilely condemns! If he ever compiles a work on England, I dare say he will announce that Charles I. was sentenced to death by the Quakers.

[47] It almost equals Broughton Brandenburg's "The Menace of the Red Flag" (Broadway Magazine, June 1908), in which Bakunin is called a Frenchman! I read the unlimited number of errors in this article with uncontrollable amazement. Few men, I said, are gifted with such an infinite amount of ignorance and godliness. The next day the newspapers announced that this same Saint Broughtonius had been arrested by his wife and was being sued for abandonment and non-support.

P. S. As I correct these proofs I learn that Brandenburg the Blessed is again under arrest; this time for forging Grover Cleveland's signature to a campaign article and selling it to the New York Times for $200.

[48] For an impartial discussion of the various anarchial schools, including of course Peter Kropotkin's, see "Anarchism" by Dr. Paul Eltzbacher.

culture, August 1890). If nations would follow this book, how great would be their gain in prosperity and happiness![49]

This book is a plea for intensive agriculture, and in view of the great cry, "Back to the land!" which is sweeping over the nations, it is a fulfilled prophecy. It is the remedy for social ills—the solution of the labor problem. Kropotkin shows that by the new method of scientific farming, a man can make a living from an acre of ground,[50] and as soon as the workingman realizes this fact—and can get a bit of land—he will be able to discharge his employer and bounce his boss. By all means read the chapters on *The Possibilities of Agriculture*: no fairy-tale is more miraculous.[51]

In 1899 appeared in book form the *Memoirs of a Revolutionist* which had first run serially in the *Atlantic Monthly*, (September 1898 to September 1899), under the title, *Autobiography of a Revolutionist*. In the magazine, the introduction is by Robert Erskine Ely, who was Kropotkin's host when the Russian traveled in America. In the book, however, the preface is by Brandes. Neither of these forewords is brilliant, but the latter is the worse. When we think of Norway, we think of only one man—Ibsen. When we think of Denmark, we think of only one man—Brandes. But in this case his preface was a fizzle. In fact, it is almost as bad as the erudite Lavrov's preface to Stepniak's splendid *Underground Russia*. No better and nobler book than these *Memoirs* has been written; nothing higher and purer could be written. Only one thing is lacking; indeed, it is the chief omission in the cosmos of Kropotkin—the poetic note. He is good and great, but the passionate fire is denied him. His soul is not aflame with poesy's burning brand. He could never cry

---

[49] Without venturing my own opinion, I must say that in this work Kropotkin enunciates a theory which few radicals accept—the Decentralisation of Industries. Briefly stated, the doctrine is this: It is untrue that certain nations are specialised either for industry or for agriculture. Countries which economists have declared to be merely agricultural lands, have recently advanced so rapidly in industries that the supremacy of the champions is seriously threatened. No one or two nations can again secure a monopoly of industry, for the tendency of modern civilization is towards a spreading and scattering of industries all over the earth. Not a mere shifting of the center of gravity from one country to another, as formerly happened in Europe when the commercial hegemony migrated from Italy to Spain, then to Holland, and finally to Britain, but an actual and permanent decentralisation of industry, by its very nature making it impossible for any nation to gain industrial ascendancy. Even the most backward nations will soon manufacture almost everything they need. There is much advantage in this combination of industrial with agricultural pursuits. It is well to have production for home use—each region producing and consuming its own manufactured goods and its own agricultural product.——Of course the Socialists are diametrically opposed to this contention, and they answer it with one word—the trusts.—When I spoke with Leonard D. Abbott about Kropotkin, he told me his high opinion of him, but soon referred to this hypothesis, and laughed. It was the same when I mentioned the point to Dr. Antoinette Konikov, etc. See Abbott's "A Visit to Prince Kropotkin," (Twentieth Century, October 2, 1897).

[50] My friend Elmer Littlefield has demonstrated the same thing on his acre on Fellowship Farm, Westwood, Mass. His magazine, Ariel, is an enthusiastic advocate of intensive agriculture.

[51] Bolton Hall's "Three Acres and Liberty" is based to a great extent on this work of Kropotkin's.

out like the student Ivan Kalayev, "My soul is burning with stormy passion; my heart is full of battle-boldness. O, if I could only see the coming of liberty! O, to pull the mask of falsehood from the face of the murderer, to strike the tyrant with the steel-arm! Enuf tears! Let the glorious, victorious struggle arise! The people are calling us! It is a shame, it is a crime to wait longer! Fall upon the enemy, my honest hereditary sword! I am thine, altogether thine, O my country, my mother!" But leaving divine enthusiasm aside, this volume is perfection. He who peruses its loving pages, gains a tender brother whose body is unseen, but whose memory becomes imperishable. When you read it, you cry a little, because the man who wrote it was so kind. Across the miles you seem to hear his fraternal voice, and you know if you write to him, he will answer you thus: "Dear Comrade." — If you have time to read but a single volume a year, and desire one by a Russian, and ask my advice, I say: Read one of these — *Underground Russia*, by Stepniak; or *Memoirs of a Revolutionist*, by Kropotkin.[52]

In 1902 he wrote *Modern Science and Anarchism*, a booklet of about one hundred pages which is much admired and extensively advertised by the anarchists.

By far his most important work of recent years is, *Mutual Aid: A Factor in Evolution*.[53] His contention is that in progressive evolution, mutual aid plays a greater part than mutual struggle. He claims that most Darwinians have misinterpreted Darwin's ideas. For an able analysis of this great book, see the review by Professor Vladimir G. Simkhovitch, (*Popular Science Quarterly*, December 1903).

In 1905 appeared his *Russian Literature*[54] — a very good and useful text-book — which originated in a series of eight lectures, delivered March 1901, at the Lowell Institute in Boston. It is not perfect, but this is not the author's fault. With only three hundred pages at his disposal, it is impossible to treat all adequately, while some writers had to be omitted entirely. For example, there is not a line about the famous anti-militarist novelist, Vsevolod Garshin (1855-1888), or of Simon Nadson (1862-1887), the exquisite and melancholy poet who chanted songs not at sunrise, but in shadow and solitude, and died in youth and sadness, leaving to the Outcasts of the Ages another great name to cherish.[55]

In reading this book we experience a peculiarly uneasy sensation: —

We read of Lomonosov, by far the greatest Russian of his age, whose life was broken by political persecution.

We read of the moral Novikov, whom Catherine II. sentenced to serve fifteen

---

[52] After finishing the "Memoirs," my friend, Miss Margaret Scott wrote me: "As a system of ethical training it might be advisable to have our police lieutenants read one chapter a day of Kropotkin, while lawyers, mayors and such, should have to get thru three. Think of the mental upheaval!"

[53] Spargo the Socialist — always a vehement foe of the Anarchists — calls this "a wonderful book." See his "The Socialists."

[54] This book is not permitted in Russia — when Kellogg Durland traveled there, he had to rip off the cover and wrap the pages around his body.

[55] Several intelligent Russians tell me Nadson is their favorite poet; therefore this must be considered a serious omission. One exclaimed, "What, he writes about Fet and not Nadson!"

years in a secret cell in Schusselburg.

We read of Labzin, who wrote against corruption, and consequently was forced to end his days in exile.

We read of Radischeff—the first to point out the horrors of serfdom—who was imprisoned, deported, and died by suicide.

We read of the epoch-making Pushkin who was exiled to Kishinev at twenty, and later to Mikhailovskoye, and who escaped permanent political exile in Siberia by accident.

We read of the Byronic Lermontov who was banished to the Caucasus for writing a poem on the death of Pushkin.

We read of Ryleev, Odoevsky, Shevchenko, Griboyedov, Pisarev, Chernishevsky, whose martyrdoms I have already mentioned.

We read of the brilliant and poetic Polezhaev, who was send to the barracks when a minor and died there from consumption.

We read of the popular novelist Bestuzhev, who was exiled to Siberia and then sent to the Caucasus as a soldier.

We read of the great Gogol who suffered at the hands of the censorship.

We read of Turgenev who was arrested and exiled to his distant estates for writing a brief obituary notice of Gogol. Had it not been for his influential friends he would have gone to Siberia.

We read of Leo Tolstoy whose excellent educational experiment was violently abolished by the government, so enraging this extraordinary man that he warned Alexander II. he would shoot the first police officer who would again dare to enter his home.

We read of the high-strung Dostoyevsky who for no reason at all was sentenced to death, brought to the gibbet, pardoned there, condemned to hard labor, imprisoned, exiled, deprived of literary work, beaten with the cat-o'-nine-tails, tortured in a thousand ways, year after year, till he became a mental and physical wreck. In all the history of the human race, from the day that primitive man roamed the untamed forests, and stubbing his naked toe against a root, fell down to worship it, to placate it, to appease it, until the scientific time that a biologist like Haeckel absolutely denied the existence of god and soul,—there has been nothing more horribly cruel than the czarish treatment which the Russian government meted out to the gifted youth who produced a work in his early twenties that caused Nekrasov to cry out to Belinsky, "A new Gogol is born to us!"[56]

We read of Plescheev, one of Russia's foremost poets, who was sent as a soldier to the Orenburg region, and endured persecution for years.

We read of Mikhail Mikhailov—one of the most valued contributors to the *Sovremennik*. (The Contemporary), a wonderful periodical numbering among its contributors, Chernishevsky, Dobrolubov, Tolstoy, Nekrasov—who was condemned to hard labor in Siberia where he soon died.

[56] On this subject see "Russia and the Russians," by Edmund Noble.

We read of Ostrovsky, the Father of the Russian Drama, who was placed under police supervision as a suspect.

We read of the loving Levitov—"a pure flower of the Russian steppes"—who while a student was exiled to the far north, and later removed to Vologda where he was forced to live in complete isolation from everything intellectual and in awful poverty verging on starvation.

We read of Petropavlovsky who was early exiled to the Siberian government of Tobolsk, where he was kept many years and from which he was released only to die soon after from consumption.

We read of Saltykoff (Schedrin), the greatest of satirists, who was exiled for several years in the miserable provincial town of Vyatka.

We read of Belinsky, the greatest of critics, who fortunately died young enuf to escape the fortress. When he was dying an agent of the state-police would call from time to time to ascertain if he were still alive. Had he recovered he would have been transfered to Peter and Paul.

We read of the persecution of Palm and Potyekhin; of the years that Melshin, Korolenko, Zasodimsky, Elpatievsky, etc, spent in exile. By this time a terrible truth dawns upon the startled mind: In Romanoff's Russia, scarcely one single writer of worth has escaped imprisonment or banishment.[57] And these prophets who have been thus persecuted were not despicable rhymers like Alfred Austin, or duke-and-duchess novelists like Harold MacGrath. They were great-brained men whose mission was to uplift a nation. Had the Catherines, Nicholases, and Alexanders been less powerful, Russia would not now be the foulest blot on our skull-strewn earth.[58]

---

[57] "The history of Russian Literature is a martyrology." See "Russian Traits and Terrors," by E. B. Lanin, the collective signature of several writers in the Fortnightly Review. The Twentieth Century (June 26, 1897) ends its review of this volume with this sentence: "Concerning Russian prisons the book makes revelations so sickening that language is polluted by the recital of them. Swinburne's fierce ode is mild in its characterization of their brutal infamy, and it is possible, after reading these pages to agree with Ernest Belfort Bax's assertion that any sane man, knowing the facts, who pronounces it wrong to assassinate the Czar, deliberately lies."—Swinburne's poem, "Russia: An Ode," altho it contains a few weak lines, is certainly one of the most fiery outbursts in the language, and is clearly the work of a master. Here is a representative passage:

> "Hell recoils heart-stricken: horror worse than hell
> Darkens earth and sickens heaven; life knows the spell,
> Shudders, quails, and sinks—or, filled with fierier breath,
> Rises red in arms devised of darkling death.
> Pity mad with passion, anguish mad with shame,
> Call aloud on justice by her darker name;
> Love grows hate for love's sake; life takes death for guide.
> Night hath none but one red star—Tyrannicide."

[58] Imagine the United States of America if Franklin had been murdered, if Irving had been knouted, if Bryant had been exiled, if Emerson had been imprisoned, if Longfellow had been starved, if Whittier had been hanged, if Holmes had been flogged, if Thoreau had been shot, if Whitman had been poisoned, if Hawthorne had been chained with iron, if

Ivan Federof was the first of Russian printers. In 1564 he cast the Slavonic characters. Being accused of heresy, he fled for his life. The Lithuanian magnates with whom he sought refuge, forced him to till the soil. Unhappy Federof said, "It was not my work to sow the grain, but to scatter thru the earth food for the mind, nourishment for the souls of all mankind." He perished in Lemberg in extreme poverty.[59] Woful was his fate—symbolic of the sad destiny which was to befall every literary man in Knoutland.[60]

Let the Russian who intends to become an author prepare his last will and testament, and notify the nearest undertaker. No night will be too dark to keep gendarmes from bursting into his room and hauling him off to a prison from which he may never emerge. (If he comes from an aristocratic family let him adopt an empty-eyed skull and yellow cross-bones as a suitable coat-of-arms). In the den of the bloody bear there is a blackness as of many clouds. Within this deep shadow, Virtue is slaughtered and Genius treated like an unwelcome cur.

Lowell had been kept in a secret dungeon, if Motley had spent his life in a mine, if Parkman had been tortured, etc., etc., etc.

[59] See "Russian Novelists" by Viscount Vogue. But the statements of this virulent French reactionary must be received with extreme caution as his perverted brains frequently prevent him from stating the truth. For example, in speaking of Turgenev, he says, "But, tho always ready to help others, he certainly never gave his aid to any political intriguer. Was it natural that a man of his refinement and high culture should have aided the schemes of wild and fruitless political conspiracies?" By 'political intriguer' he means an 'enemy to the empire, a revolutionist. Now the facts are that no one was of greater use to Herzen the arch-revolutionist and his thundering Kolokol, than Turgenev. Herzen was in England and often it was impossible to explain how he knew some of the events which he described. It was Turgenev who furnished him this information. All this is revealed by the published correspondence of Herzen and Turgenev. Turgenev was fully and entirely in sympathy with the Russian Revolution. He earnestly desired to meet Ippolit Mishkin, and begged Kropotkin to tell him all he knew about this defiant revolutionary orator. Turgenev deeply loved his own Bazaroff, and in explaining him says, "If the reader is not won by Bazaroff, notwithstanding his roughness, absence of heart, pitiless dryness and terseness, then the fault is with me—I have missed my aim; but to sweeten him with syrup (to use Bazaroff's own language), this I did not want to do, altho perhaps thru that I would have won Russian youth at once to my side.... When he calls himself nihilist, you must read revolutionist."

[60] This does not include obsequious authors like Derzhavin and Karamzin. Masters are usually willing to fling a few crumbs to their fawning dogs.

IN LATER LIFE

There are at this moment only two great Russians who think
for the Russian people, and whose thoughts belong to mankind, —
Leo Tolstoy and Peter Kropotkin. — Georg Brandes.

A storm careered madly over the Northern Sea, its impatient waves heaving and howling, leaping with a burning frenzy, the fuming raging billows surging and swelling, calling and crying, roaring louder and louder, vaulting higher and higher.

The steamer shook and swayed and struggled; the frightened passengers sought shelter in their state-rooms, but one of them sat for hours upon the stem of the deck, enjoying the tempest intensely, putting out his face so it could be watered by the foam of the dashing waves. This was Kropotkin. After the years he had spent in the charnel cell, no wonder every fibre in his body was trembling and throbbing to meet the force and passion of the sea-storm.

He landed safely in the country where Herzen founded *The Bell*, where Lavrov edited *Forward*, where Felix Volkhovsky was to conduct *Free Russia*, and where he himself was to start *Freedom*.

For over thirty years he has remained abroad. He never returned to Russia. He is one of the few revolutionists who never went back to that sunken swamp where liberty's wrapped in her winding-sheets, while tyranny's robed in ermine. There are two reasons for this. In the first place he became interested in a new-born idea — Anarchism — and felt he could be more useful as an apostle of this movement than as a rebel in Trepovdom. As is well-known, his lectures and writings on the subject have earned him the title, "Father of Anarchist-Communism." Secondly, when the Nihilists were changed (by purple butchers) into Terrorists, they dropped their propaganda of pamphlets to study the properties of petroleum, and thus were forced to neglect the varletry. However, Kropotkin's sympathies drew him more and more towards those human machines who toil so hard for their bread that if you cut their pennies open, the blood would gush from them.

About a year after his escape, Kropotkin attended an important labor congress in Belgium (1877). A few days later the police received an order to arrest him. At this time the theologians were in power, and the Belgian comrades knowing a clerical ministry would be only too willing to turn him over to the blood-sucking czar, insisted upon his leaving the country. On returning to his hotel, he found his good friend James Guillaume — small physically, big in all other respects — barring the way to his room, and sternly announcing that Kropotkin could enter only by using force against him.

The next morning the ejected delegate sailed for London, but soon went to Paris where he helped to form radical groups. Again he was wanted by the police, but by mistake they arrested a Russian student (1878). Later he left for Switzerland where he founded an anarchistic paper, *Le Revolte* (1879).

Two years later Alexander II. was assassinated. The government hanged the revolutionists at home, but pretended the exiles abroad were responsible for the deed. The Holy League was formed to execute the refugees. An officer who knew Kropotkin when he was a page de chambre, was appointed to kill him. A woman was sent from Petersburg to Geneva to lead the conspiracy. Kropotkin took matters coolly, collected a pile of threatening letters—of which the police later relieved him—and nothing happened except that Helvetia was told if it did not expel the agitator, then Alexander III., the Lord's Anointed, would drive out from Russia all the Swiss governesses and ladies' maids, while the czarina would refuse to eat Swiss cheese. This was more than the little republic could stand, and Kropotkin was told to go. He says he did not take umbrage at this.

He went once more to London, where he met his old comrade Chaykovsky, and together they began to preach their gospel of freedom. Always to work for the liberation of humanity—that isn't such a bad idea, is it?[61]

At this time there was no movement in the Island which had imbibed the narcotic of reaction and lay in a wakeless torpor, and Kropotkin and his devoted wife felt so lonely among the napping Britons that they decided to cross the channel. "Better a prison in France than this grave," they said. They were followed by an army of informers, freely furnished by the loving Russian Government which cannot bear to see its children travel without suitable protection. Not to be outdone in courtesy, the French police soon escorted him to the official lodging-house.

Kropotkin was incarcerated in the central prison of Clairvaux where had been confined old Blanqui—the communard at whose burial Louise Michel spoke words which will have no funeral. Kropotkin was well-treated, the officials were polite, and he was permitted to give his fellow-prisoners instruction in physics, languages, geometry and cosmography. Unfortunately, Clairvaux is built on marshy ground, and Kropotkin fell sick from malaria. His wife who was studying in Paris, preparing for the degree of Doctor of Science, hastened from Wurtz's laboratory to the prison-town. She remained there until her iconoclast was released. This event occurred after three years' imprisonment. He then went to the capital, lectured to an audience of several thousand, and left France immediately to avoid a forcible expulsion.

---

[61] Kropotkin is still able to cross London Bridge, but his comrade is missing. For many years Chaykovsky kept away from Russia. During a whole generation the man who taught Perovskaya was a wanderer in other lands. Some months ago he went back—he could control his yearning no longer. He is now in the Fortress of Peter and Paul. The Father of the Revolution will sleep among his children.

P. S. As this book goes to press, the happy news comes that Chaykovsky has been liberated on a heavy bail, but it is not yet known what the government intends to do with him.

The Cossacks

Indulging in a favorite Russian pastime.

Such are some of the scenes in the life of Peter Kropotkin—imprisoned by governments, pursued by police, followed by spies,[62] hounded by agents of autocracy.

This peace-loving man whose name is synonym for kindness, this tender soul as modest as Newton, as gentle as Darwin, has been hunted from frontier to border-line. Against none of his persecutors does he utter a single invective. He is the epitome of mildness, the incarnation of humaneness.[63]

Ask anyone who has seen Kropotkin for an hour or has known him for a generation, to describe his most characteristic trait, and the invariable answer will be: simplicity. His is a great spirit—it has cast out flam. "Kropotkin is one of the most sincere and frank of men," says Stepniak. "He always says the truth, pure and simple, without any regard for the *amour propre* of his hearers, or for any consideration whatever. This is the most striking and sympathetic feature of his character. Every word he says may be absolutely believed. His sincerity is such, that sometimes in the ardour of discussion an entirely fresh consideration unexpectedly presents itself to his mind, and sets him thinking. He immediately stops, remains quite absorbed for a moment, and then begins to think aloud, speaking as tho he were an opponent. At other times he carries on this discussion mentally, and after some moments of silence, turning to his astonished adversary, smilingly says, 'You are right.' This absolute sincerity renders him the best of friends, and gives especial weight to his praise and blame."

Most of Kropotkin's Russian revolutionary comrades—using the term Comrade in its broad sense—ended their days in misery. Kroutikoff strangled himself with a piece of linen; Stransky poisoned himself; Zapolsky cut his throat with a pair of scissors; Leontovitch and Bogomoloff hacked theirs with a bit of glass; Zhutin died in chains bound to the wall; Kolenkin perished from wounds torn open by fetters; Rodin poisoned himself with matches; Nathalie Armfeldt died of prison consumption; Beverly was wounded with bullets and murdered with bayonet-thrusts; Ivan Cherniavsky and wife and child were transported to Irkutsk, the temperature was thirty degrees below zero, and the baby died, while the mother went mad, howled, laughed, prayed, cursed, rocked the dead infant in her arms and sang nursery songs;[64] Semyonovsky shot himself; Uspensky hanged himself; Martinova was dragged to the police station on the very day that she expected to become a mother; Gratchevsky threw kerosene from his lamp over himself, set it on fire and died shrieking—but at least he escaped from Schlusselburg; Edelson was marched to the Arctic zone even after he had become insane; Mukhanov was killed with a volley of balls; Sergius Pik was struck in the head, his jaw was

[62] Some types are depicted in Gorky's latest work, "The Spy," translated by Thomas Seltzer. Because of its subject-matter this book acts as an emetic.

[63] I remember hearing James F. Morton, A. M.—author of the excellent essay "The Curse of Race Prejudice"—speak to Elbert Hubbard about Catherine Breshkovskaya whom he had seen at the Sunrise Club, and in wishing to illustrate her gentleness and lack of resentment for those who ill-treated her, he called her "a female Kropotkin."

[64] When George Kennan heard this woman's story, his face became wet with tears almost for the first time since boyhood. See his admirable but terrible "Siberia and the Exile System."

smashed by the gendarmes' guns, a ghastly hole was made above his eye, his blood and brains oozed and fell on his chest;[65] Sophia Gurevitch was ripped open with bayonets; Sherstnova was shot to death for signaling with a hand-mirror; the young wife of Felix Volkhovsky shot herself thru the head; the wonderful Kuprianov died in prison at the age of nineteen; Shtchedrin was chained to the barrow, became insane and so perished; Nadyeshda Sigida was flogged to death;[66] Marie Vetrova was raped and murdered;[67] Jessy Helfman was tortured indescribably; Bobohov swallowed a handful of opium; Ossinsky's hair turned white in five minutes; Maria Kovalevskaya—cover thy face, freedom—suffered, took poison and died in the prison infirmary; Yakimova stayed up nights in the Trubetzkoi Ravelin to prevent the rats from devouring her baby; Olga Lubatovitch was stripped naked by men and beaten; Malyovany died in exile; the student Schmidt was murdered in his cell by his jailers; Spiridonova was violated by a cossack officer and by a police chief; the high-minded Plotnikoff ended his days in an asylum; Bogulubov became a raving lunatic; Serdukov was so broken that he shot himself after his release; the poet Polivanoff also committed suicide thus—(Ah, those twenty long years in Schlusselburg!); the noble Balmaschoff was hanged; the beautiful Zinaida too; Isaiev, Okladsky, Zubkovsky went mad; Kviotkovsky, Presniakoff, Soukanoff died in Skipper Peter's Prison; Buzinsky, Gellis, Ignatius Ivanoff succumbed in the Key-Town Fortress; to Federoff was reserved a fate worse than death, worse than torture, worse than madness, for it was his destiny to become a dupe of the Black Hundreds and unwittingly slay Georg Iollos—lover of liberty;[68] Ludmila Volkenstein,—but why continue an unhappy list which has neither beginning nor end? I could fill a library with such cases.

Such individual torments fell not to the lot of Peter Kropotkin. Personally he has been favored by fortune. He has touched existence on every side and lived every life. The wisdom of the world is in his brain, and within his heart is lodged all its goodness. His experience has been unusually wide. He has been on intimate terms with czar and serf, he has met millionaire and mendicant, he has hobnobbed with prince and pauper. He has lectured to aristocratic audiences who gazed calmly at him thru gilded lorgnettes and foppish monocles, and to empty-stomached workmen who cried loudly, "Pierre! Pierre! Notre Pierre!"[69]

---

[65] See the letter by the eye-witness Nicholas Zotoff (hanged August 7, 1889). It is published in "King Stork and King Log," a two-volume work by Stepniak.

[66] Leo Deutsch was a prisoner at Kara at the time of this tragedy, and he describes it in his "Sixteen Years in Siberia."

[67] See "Woman, the Glory of the Russian Revolution" (Altruria, July 1907), by Dr. Sonia Winstan. Note this sentence: "In arrests the police are always more cruel to women than to men, and I have seen women dragged by the hair to jail thru the streets of St. Petersburg, while men in the same group were led along in the ordinary way. In the prisons innocent young women are often placed with the lowest murderers."

[68] In Robert Crozier Long's "The Black Hundreds," in The Cosmopolitan, January 1908.

[69] "He is an incomparable agitator. Gifted with a ready and eager eloquence, he becomes all passion when he mounts the platform. Like all true orators, he is stimulated by the sight of the crowd which is listening to him. Upon the platform this man is transformed.

The finest men of all nations have honored him. When a prisoner at Clairvaux, a petition for his release was signed by such geniuses as Herbert Spencer, Victor Hugo and Algernon Swinburne. When he required books, Ernest Renan put his library at his service. While at Paris, Turgenev—who won immortality by a single word—wished to be introduced to him and celebrate his escape by a little banquet. When Catherine Breshkovskaya journeyed for the first time to Petersburg, Kropotkin was on the same train; they discussed problems, and this extraordinary woman says his words thrilled like fire.[70] Elie Reclus was his brother. Elisee published his writings and asked him to contribute to his Geography—the greatest in existence. Jean Grave is his disciple. Ernest Crosby loved him. Georg Brandes praises him lavishly. Zola paid his work a high compliment. Elizabeth Cady Stanton spent an interesting day at his home. J. Scott Keltie, the eminent authority on African history, is one of his warmest friends. Bates, the Naturalist on the Amazons whom Darwin mentions so often, appreciated his scientific ability. Enrico Ferri closely studied his works. The learned Lavrov was his comrade. Denjiro Kotoku, the Japanese essayist who founded the radical *Heiminshimbun*, considers him one of the greatest humanitarians of the nineteenth century.[71] At the home of Edward Clodd he argued with Grant Allen. When at East Aurora, I saw only one picture over the desk of Elbert Hubbard, and that was Kropotkin. Those who have read *De Profundis* will recall in what high pure words Oscar Wilde speaks of him. Tolstoy calls him a learned man.[72] The authors of *Russian Traits and Terrors* speak of him as "one whose scientific accuracy and objectivity is beyond praise." James Knowles so respected him that he allowed him to write anarchistic articles for his high-toned *Nineteenth Century*. Laurence Gronlound gives him as a type of

He trembles with emotion; his voice vibrates with that accent of profound conviction, not to be mistaken or counterfeited, and only heard when it is not merely the mouth which speaks, but the innermost heart. His speeches, altho he cannot be called an orator of the first rank, produce an immense impression; for when feeling is so intense it is communicative, and electrifies an audience. When, pale and trembling, he descends from the platform, the whole room throbs with applause."—STEPNIAK.

[70] In Ernest Poole's "Catherine Breshkovskaya" in the Outlook. See also Kennan. After being a Siberian exile for over twenty-two years she came to America to collect funds for the Revolution, and immediately went back to Russia. She was captured, and like Chaykovsky is now in the fortress of Peter and Paul. She often said it was a shame for a Revolutionist to die in bed.

[71] In my "Symposium on Humanitarians." For several other contributors who mentioned Kropotkin as one of their favorites, see this "Symposium," now published in book form by The Altrurians.

[72] In the "Russian Revolution," a senseless pamphlet, edited by V. Tchertkoff who is talented enuf to be doing better things. When it comes to a question of righteous resistance, Leo Tolstoy is unbearable. A man who can say in effect, "Let the officials do whatever they want to do, let them shoot you down as often as they please, let them fill every prison in vast Russia with your bodies, let them rape your mothers and daughters and wives, let them hang your young children, but never resist in any way, only think of Jesus and read the Gospels,"—such a man is what the doctors call non compos mentis. No wonder the Russian Government does not molest him. The gentle Kropotkin says, "I am in sympathy with most of Tolstoy's work, tho there are many of his ideas with which I absolutely disagree—his asceticism, for instance, and his doctrine of non-resistance. It seems to me, too, that he has bound himself, without reason or judgment, to the letter of the New Testament."

the ideal anarchist. In the soul of every libertarian swings a fragrant censer which offers up olibanum to the stainless character of the great revolutionist. Put those who love Kropotkin on one side, and those who don't on the other, and you will have separated the heralds of the morning from the spooks of the night. It is no more necessary to be an anarchist-communist to have a warm spot in your heart for Peter Kropotkin, than it is necessary to believe in Adam and Eve to enjoy Milton's *Paradise Lost*.

THE HISTORIAN OF THE REVOLUTION

The heroism of our Russian comrades in the face of torture and death will be told in days to come by generations made rich by their sacrifices. History will pay an eternal homage to the victims of the bloody tyranny which now rules Russia.—J. Ramsay MacDonald, M. P.

 o the present generation of Russian Revolutionists Kropotkin is not an influence, but an inspiration. He is not a leader but an elder brother. He is to them a type of the man who without a moment's hesitation leaves everything for the Cause. He is a powerful voice crying out loudly against the oppressors of mankind. Voices like these they hear distinctly, and follow eagerly, tho they lead to a cold Siberian grave.

With the lavishness of the mountain cataract that wastes its waters on the rocks, the young radicals of Russia pour out their blood for an ignorant[73] and ungrateful people. As willingly as lovers walk to the altar, they go to the slaughter. They die as serenely as if they had a thousand lives to lose instead of one. When a Revolutionist is hanged, another takes his place while the gallow-grass around the choked neck is still visible. Imprison them for a quarter of a century, and on the day of their release they will conspire against czardom.[74] Torture them in the mines of Nerchinsk, beat the men with the plet, rape the girls at will, thrust them into black holes swarming with vermin and rodents, taunt them, starve them, chill them, strike them to the ground, stamp on their faces with military boots, deprive them of air, worry their nerves to the breaking-point, string them up on slippery scaffolds, and they will only shout, "Long live the Revolution!"[75]

Liberty is the goddess they worship, and for her sake, when necessary, they taste no food by day and touch no pillow by night. For her they put away books

---

[73] See "The Laborer and the Man with the White Hand" in Turgenev's "Poems in Prose."

[74] Since they are not permitted to work for freedom from the house-tops, they must do it in their secret chambers.

[75] For a Russian revolutionary drama powerfully depicting such a scene, see "On the Eve," by Dr. Leopold Kampf. It has no connection with Turgenev's great novel of the same name. For a tragedy whose interest centers around a beautiful young man who has become insane in a Russian prison, see "To the Stars," by Leonid Andreyev, (Translated by Dr. A. Goudiss, Poet Lore, Winter 1907). Called by Helen A. Clarke, "a play in which there is no villain except the far-off Russian Government."

and handle bombs, and exchange palaces for prisons, and leave desks for dungeons, and go from colleges to coffins. Their backs are ready for the lash, their throats are prepared for the noose.

If the end comes at dawn in the yard of the Schlusselburg Prison, or at noon below the level of the Neva in the Fortress of Peter and Paul, or at midnight among the silent snows of Saghalien,—O liberty, how thy lovers meet it!

Against an autocracy as powerful as the Romanoff dynasty, rebels have never before contended. In all the world no men and women like those of Young Russia. From primal days to modern times, no martyrs like these. Such sacrifices were never seen before.[76] Few expect to live beyond twenty, and thousands upon thousands perish long before that age.[77] They offer themselves to be nipped in the fairest hour of their proudest bloom. O brilliant-eyed youth, O rosy-cheeked maid, be not so heedless of yourselves. Think a little of the pleasures of life. Leave the stupid muzhik to his fate, and cross the sea to a freer land.

But from the foot of the scaffold there comes a cry, and from the steppes of Siberia is heard a voice, and from the saltworks of Usolie rings an answer, and from the gold-mines of Kara comes a response, and from the Butirki of Moscow someone speaks, and from the prison of Akatui, Young Russia utters the same word—Svoboda! Svoboda! Svoboda!

Sometime in the future, when the true historian of the Russian Revolution appears, he will write of men and women of so exalted a nature, that antiquity will be dumb and boast no more her classic heroes.

He will write of Bakunin, the Jupiter from whose forehead leaped a full-

---

[76] "Since the world's first wail went up from lands and seas
　　Ears have heard not, tongues have told not things like these.
　　Dante, led by love's and hate's accordant spell
　　Down the deepest and the loathiest ways of hell,
　　Where beyond the brook of blood the rain was fire,
　　Where the scalps were masked with dung more deep than mire,
　　Saw not, where filth was foulest, and the night
　　Darkest, depths whose fiends could match the Muscovite.
　　Set beside this truth, his deadliest vision seems
　　Pale and pure and painless as a virgin's dreams.
　　Maidens dead beneath the clasping lash, and wives
　　Rent with deadlier pangs than death—for shame survives,
　　Naked, mad, starved, scourged, spurned, frozen, fallen, deflowered,
　　Souls and bodies as by fangs of beasts devoured.
　　Sounds that hell would hear not, sights no thoughts could shape,
　　Limbs that feel as flame the ravenous grasp of rape," etc.

Swinburne: "Russia: An Ode."

[77] "Marie Spiridonova was only twenty-one when she killed Lujenovsky; and in St. Petersburg I knew a girl, a medical student—sweet, quiet, all soul—who was barely eighteen when she said to me, simply "I shall live but a year or two—no more." In this expectancy of death there is no mawkishness, no pose. They have seen their comrades go after a few days or years of service; their fate will be the same." LeRoy Scott, "The Terrorists," in Everybody's Magazine.

fledged movement;

Of Dobroluboff, the genius who perished at twenty-five with a vaster wisdom to his credit than any youngster of whom we have record;

Of Olga Lubatovitch, the immortal girl in whose great heart burnt the undying fire of insurrection;

Of Vera Figner, the poetess, a woman of the rarest beauty and the highest talents, who passed her life behind stone walls;

Of Aaron Sundelevitch, the thoughtful Jew who established the first free printing press in Saint Petersburg;

Of Zuckerman, who was so merry that even in hell he jested, but who after all was only human and committed suicide in the wilds of Yakutsk;

Of Maria Kutitonskaya, who was ready to be hanged with a baby in her womb;

Of Eugene Semyonovsky, who wrote a letter to his father before committing suicide, that would make everything on earth—except of course an official—weep;

Of the taciturn Kibalchitch, who was arrested for giving a pamphlet to a peasant, and who, hearing in prison that an attempt had been made to exterminate the imperial family, broke his habitual silence by exclaiming, "It's good! It's fine! If they don't send me to Siberia, I'll study nitroglycerine,"—and who kept his promise, for he was the chemist who prepared the bomb that caused the blood of Alexander to redden the snow;

Of Ippolit Mishkin, the hero of the Case where all were heroes, whose oratory inflamed all Russia, who was sentenced because he tried to rescue Chernishevsky, who received fifteen additional years for making a speech in prison over the dead body of Comrade Leo Dmohovsky, a man whom Turgenev wished to know, and whom Perovskaya wished to save;

Of Demetrius Lisogub, the millionaire who lived like a pauper, giving everything to the Cause and spending nothing on himself, grudging every coin he had to pay for his bread, dressing in rags even during the severest winters, supporting for a time the whole revolutionary movement, but continually sorrowing that in order not to forfeit his wealth he could take no active part in the battle, and smiling with happiness only when brought to the scaffold in the hangman's cart, for at last he could bestow more than money—he could sacrifice himself;

Of the printer Maria Kriloff who tho old, ill and half-blind, worked with so much devotion that she excelled young and strong compositors, and who stuck to her post until she was arrested, weapons in hand, in the secret printing-office of *Cherny Perediel*;

Of the intrepid Sophia Bogomoletz, who left husband and child for the Revolution, and spent her life in prison;

Of Nicholas Blinoff, who was slaughtered in the Jewish pogrom in Zhitomir with the word 'Brother' on his noble lips;

Of young Leo Weinstein, who fell in the same massacre crying 'Comrades;'

Of the child Silin of Warsaw, who when only fifteen years of age was condemned to death; when he was led out with bandaged eyes to be shot on the sand-hills, he wept so bitterly that the soldiers called to him, "Do not cry, there is no pain," upon which he shouted back, "I am crying because I must die before accomplishing anything."

He will tell how Valerian Ossinsky died, and then we will not think of Christ upon the Cross.

He will write of those soft-eyed, sweet-voiced, tender Terrorists whose blessed bombs and bullets laid tyrants low: Zinaida who shot Min; Spiridonova who slew Lujenovsky; Bizenko who killed Sakharoff; Eserskaja who assassinated Klingenberg; Ragozinnikova who destroyed Maximoffsky.

Of those noble and daring youths who struck to the death their country's oppressors: Kaltourin and Gelvakov who dispatched Strelnikoff; Balmaschoff who executed Sipyagin; Karpowitch who ended the days of Bogolepoff; Kalayev who removed Sergius; Schaumann who aimed well at Bobrikoff; Sazonov who wiped out Plehve.

Of these he will write and of many, many more whose names are unknown to an ignorant public which yells itself hoarse for empty-headed officials, but whose memories encircle the hearts of freedom's orphans.

He will write too, of a revolutionary thinker who dreams a philosophy which would dethrone tyranny and upraise liberty, the humanitarian who harbors a love which reaches to the uttermost ends of the earth, the true World-Man of the Better-Day—Comrade Kropotkin.

Lector House believes that a society develops through a two-fold approach of continuous learning and adaptation, which is derived from the study of classic literary works spread across the historic timeline of literature records. Therefore, we aim at reviving, repairing and redeveloping all those inaccessible or damaged but historically as well as culturally important literature across subjects so that the future generations may have an opportunity to study and learn from past works to embark upon a journey of creating a better future.

This book is a result of an effort made by Lector House towards making a contribution to the preservation and repair of original ancient works which might hold historical significance to the approach of continuous learning across subjects.

HAPPY READING & LEARNING!

LECTOR HOUSE LLP
E-MAIL: lectorpublishing@gmail.com